WOW!
Resumes for
Creative Careers

WOW!
Resumes for
Creative Careers

Matthew J. De Luca

Nanette F. De Luca

McGraw-Hill

New York San Francisco Washington, D.C. Auckland Bogotá
Caracas Lisbon London Madrid Mexico City Milan
Montreal New Delhi San Juan Singapore
Sydney Tokyo Toronto

Library of Congress Cataloging-in-Publication Data

DeLuca, Matthew J.
    WOW! : resumes for creative careers / Matthew J. DeLuca.
      p. cm.
    Includes index.
    ISBN 0-07-016381-2
    1. Resumes (Employment)   I. Ttile.
HF5383.D43   1997
808'.06665–dc21   97–9589
                                              CIP

McGraw-Hill

*A Division of The **McGraw·Hill** Companies*

   2 3 4 5 6 7 8 9 0 MAL/MAL 9 0 2 1 0 9 8

ISBN 0-07-016381-2 (pbk.)

The sponsoring editor for this book was Betsy Brown, the assistant editor was Danielle Bauer, the editing supervisor was Fred Dahl, and the production supervisor was Tina Cameron. It was set in Stone Serif by Inkwell Publishing Services.

Printed and bound by Malloy Lithography.

Contents

Preface

This book is designed to help you—the creative person—apply your creativity to the job search process to make it a completely effective by starting with the design of a terrific resume.

Don Tapscott, in his new book *The Digital Economy*, states that, *"The new economy is ... knowledge economy based on the application of human know-how to everything we produce and how we produce it. In the new economy, more and more of the economy's added value will be created by brain rather than brawn* [page 7].*"* This is a time that emphasizes the knowledge worker. What a perfect time for those of you, whose jobs and careers require your creativity and particular expertise, to be looking. At the same time, though, you need to become a "product." From your first contact you need to demonstrate that you are an astute job applicant who exudes creativity and puts a premium on the thinking process in everything you do. What better place is there to start making this lasting impression than in your resume.

This book takes you through the process of drafting a resume. It enables you to become a more effective applicant from the very start of your search through the job offer itself.

Matthew J. De Luca
Nanette F. De Luca

Acknowledgments

As we work with Philip Ruppel and Betsy Brown on book project after book project, the germination of the creative process takes a different form each time. In this instance a casual comment about recruiting for creative positions at Titan Sports, Inc. to Phillip led to a few brief conversations with Betsy, and a book filling a missing niche was born.

The second part of this process was the discussion to make this a joint project. We appreciate the confidence both Philip and Betsy had in our belief that a joint effort would lead to a far superior product. Among the individuals who helped in the spirit and content of this book were Bobbie Lyons from Lee Hecht Harrison—as imaginative and creative a career consultant (and mucn more) as any we have been fortunate to meet; Debbie Bonnanzio, the head of Creative Services at Titan Sports, Inc. who is a day-to-day inspiration with her continuing need to meet the demands of Titan Sports (and the World Wrestling Federation) by finding creative individuals from a variety of professions; and Vince and Linda McMahon who continue to provide the human resource challenges and opportunities that only a world class organization in the entertainment industry is truly capable of. Also to be mentioned is Palma Mitchell who finds in all the positions and the individuals she meets in the execution of her Human Resource responsibilities a truly creative side.

Thanks to the many individuals who provided information on their professions, who shared their resumes with us, who gave us insight into the myriad details of many jobs, and who guided us in the intricacies of the Internet and job-searching on-line. Folks on-line, particularly 'Viners on Pipeline's Grapevine, were always forthcoming with encouragement, as well as information about software and about the Internet. This was truly a group effort and appreciation goes to Bill Blum, Chelsey Carter of *CareerWEB*, Michelle De Luca, Lauren De Luca, Susan Howie, Valerie M. Kameya, Marie-Elaine Monti, Brad Neff (Internet Sleuth), Marvin E. Newman, D. J. O'Neil, Cindy O'Neil, Marisa Palmisano, Rick Panson (The Duplex), *Television Food Network* Staff, Gary Resnikoff of Career Magazine, Peter Rippon, David Rodman, Sukey Rosenbaum, Shawn Spengler—President of InPursuit, and Kathy Wallack.

All these people, experts in their own fields, helped put the WOW! in our resumes. The final touches are thanks to Fred Dahl and his staff at Inkwell Publishing Services for another book superbly edited.

WOW!
Resumes for
Creative Careers

How Resumes for Creative Jobs *Is* Different ... And What Will Make Your Resume Stand Out from the Rest

This book is intended to help you (the creative person) to apply your creativity to the job search process, to make it a completely effective one by starting with the design of a terrific resume. The book will take you through the process of drafting a resume so that this essential job search tool makes you a more successful applicant, from the very start of your search through the job offer itself.

All professions require some creativity. The proactive employee is the one all the fad books now portray as the ideal. This is the person who uses imagination to anticipate needs and make innovative suggestions. The implication is that the opposite qualities—passivity and narrow vision—are ineffective and undesirable. While some of this talk about being proactive is no doubt silly, the ability to react and adjust to changes and altered situations is a required trait in today's turbulent work environment. Today's job applicants need to blend imagination and resourcefulness with style and substance. An interesting and attractive resume is your most effective "calling card."

This book is about creative resumes—resumes for people working in creative professions. What is a creative profession? Without defining it too narrowly, a creative profession is any in which creativity is an essential responsibility of the position. There are many professions in which creativity is at most a very minor part of the job's responsibility. Accountants, for instance, are expected to perform at standardized levels set within the profession, following generally accepted accounting principles. The practicing accountant is expected to restrain from creativity and adhere to a largely fixed system of established practices and procedures. At the auditing level, creativity is perceived as a deviation from the norm and will more likely than not represent a problem.

There are other occupations in which creativity is the most essential ingredient. Writers, for instance (whether they write for print or electronic media, entertainment, advertising, public relations, or any other industry), must look at a blank page or screen and produce words. The value they add to an organization is in filling the blank "page" with quality content.

There is a third group of occupations that are in a gray area regarding the role and importance of creativity. In this book we include as creative any positions that contribute directly to the creative side of the organization. A position as vice president responsible for creative services is included in our definition of creativity; the job of chief financial officer in the same organization is not.

Our intent is not to exclude any occupation from consideration (nor do we promise to be all-inclusive), but the focus of the book is on occupations that demand creativity as their objective. We also do not mean to suggest that for the professions included, the sample resumes portray the only career paths that could be followed.

More of "You" in Your Resume

Regardless of the profession, the resume writing process is a creative one. The more an individual concentrates on the uniqueness of his or her set of skills, values, interests, and experiences, the more creative the resulting resume will be. Many hiring managers realize that regardless of the job, the real value added by an employee is that of a knowledge (or skill) worker with a unique approach to the job. Employers are becoming increasingly sophisticated and demanding in what they require. Today's employers are usually not looking for the "same old, same old." This is particularly true for creative positions where originality is a major prerequisite. As an applicant looking for a creative job, you need to portray yourself—first through your resume and then throughout the interview and selection process—not only as accomplished and experienced, but also as someone who "can do more, and better, as only I can do it."

You have to display a spark, an attitude that says you are "dressed and ready to play." Your resume should be intriguing, so that the reader wants to learn more. Why does an employer choose one resume over another that lists similar qualifications? Some employers look for "like me/unlike me" qualities, consciously or unconsciously. Did you go to the same school as he or she, take the same courses, or appear to have the same work history? In some cases it can be just luck (unless you have an inside track and know that the employer is just wild for tennis and you mention—purposely—that you play regularly in a league) that gets your resume chosen and gets you the interview.

Looking for a new job is also an opportunity to "reinvent" yourself. Take a look at what you have done, what you enjoy doing, and what the future can offer you. A job search is an opportunity to change directions, to be more creative about what you want to do and where you want to use your talents. Many authors, such as Don Tapscott (*Digital Economy* and *Paradigm Shift*) have stated that the new economy—the economy that you are looking for a job in—is involved in a radical change due to knowledge and technology. Businesses and individuals must rely on innovation in order to succeed. For example, travel agents may be perceived as creative types: They find out what you like or don't like in vacation spots, make recommendations, get brochures for you, find hotels in your price range, check flight schedules, and deliver a complete, tailored-to-you vacation package. But if you can go on-line to surf the Net and visit hotels in real-time animation, go on a virtual visit to several Caribbean islands to see what the amenities are, and then book your own reservations and flights on-line, who needs a travel agent? Why would Marriott or TWA pay fees to agents in the future if they can market directly to the consumer? Tapscott has offered the opinion that those with jobs in the "middle," who bring together the two ends of a transaction, should do some serious career planning for the future. If knowledge is to be the prime asset of organizations in the future, then creativity must also be included. (If you are a travel agent, perhaps now is the time to investigate on-line jobs where your knowledge and creativity can be invested.)

In any job market, no one can rely on pure luck. Certainly, hope for a lucky break and be eager to seize all the opportunities presented. But while you are waiting and hoping for fate to cast the golden opportunity your way, you should be doing everything in your power to create your own golden opportunities. *You* have to get the interviews. *Your resume* must be visually inviting, intriguing, and on the mark with the qualifications needed to fill the position.

- Throughout this book you will learn through demonstration what facts to include in your resume and how to present information for all types of positions that are directly or indirectly linked to creative job opportunities.

- Specific guides will be provided for a variety of specialties, for example, arts, entertainment, and traditional as well as the new media. These tips will pinpoint specific concerns and details that are job relevant.

- Last, there are more than seventy samples of resumes for various creative jobs included for your careful consideration, regardless of your personal occupational choice. They are intended to be neither all-inclusive nor a comprehensive compilation but rather a sampling of a variety of major job categories, with representatives from a broad mix of industries as well as occupations. They are included to stimulate and influence the reader's own resume preparation: to help you recognize a good resume, identify elements for personal inclusion, and encourage and stimulate personal sensitivity to a variety of resume details for you to consider while drafting your own. Even if a sample resume is not directly related to your own profession, it may include details or layout that you find particularly attractive and appealing and that you can use in your own resume.

Resume Basics

Before proceeding further, consider the following elements of the resume process.

First, every resume has two aspects: form and content.

FORM}	visual impact, what the resume looks like	=paper =print/font =color =organization =format =graphics =verbiage

CONTENT}	factual impact, what you say and what you leave out	=grammar =jargon =information, facts =data =inferences

Influences on Form and Content

The form is the visual side of the presentation material—in all its aspects. How the resume looks, how you have organized the materials, what kind and color of paper you have chosen, how you addressed the envelope—these elements will either enhance or detract from your resume.

The content is what the words say and how they are put together. Verbs, jargon, grammar, information included (or excluded), where you have worked, what you have done, and what the employer can infer from your resume will all affect whether you receive a telephone call requesting an interview.

To be effective it is essential that you pay attention to both form and content. Ignoring or forgetting this rule will result in a resume that cannot be used effectively as a job search tool.

Second, the resume is the first tool you have available that can be used to intrigue a potential employer.

You should develop a resume that not only *convinces* the employer that you have the skills and experience needed but also *generates interest* in the reader to such an extent that he or she wants to know more about you. The resume then becomes what it should be: a marketing tool to get you an interview.

Third, for a resume to be effective it must be developed with a specific target audience in mind.

Unless the resume is *customer-driven*, the likelihood of success will be slight or none at all. Recently, a career counselor met a fellow who had taken her workshop and who was obviously frustrated. He said he had applied all the rules she suggested in the workshop but he still hadn't found success in landing a job in his chosen profession, human resources. Needing a place to start the discussion, she turned to the most obvious and asked for a copy of his resume. It didn't take her ten seconds to discover that the problem began right there. Not only were there typographical errors in the text, but the objective stated was to *"find a challenging job in either accounting or human resources"*—leaving every potential employer to wonder which job he wanted! Customer-driven resumes are geared to answer questions such as

"What can this person do for our organization?"

"What value will he or she add?"

"Why should I interview him or her?"

Three Resume Goals

In preparing a resume and looking for a job, effort is not the key, but result is. There is no scorecard in the sky that tallies the efforts of each individual job seeker, and no scorekeeper to ensure that whoever gives the most effort wins the job. In fact, for some of us, those who appear to find jobs effortlessly are a source of considerable frustration. The requirement for success is to be effective. To that end, consider the three goals of a resume:

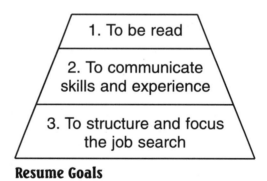

Resume Goals

Goal #1: Every resume written wants—needs—to be read. Remember that resumes don't get people jobs. People who get interviews get jobs. If the resume is discarded unread, it will never generate the invitation to meet with the hiring manager.

Goal #2: Every resume must communicate your skills, experiences, and interests. The purpose doesn't end here. The ideal outcome is to stimulate attention, motivate pursuit, **and** get you the interview.

Goal #3: Every resume should help you structure your job search and focus on your goals. The resume development process is an opportunity to consider where you have come from, what you have been doing, and how effective you have been in doing it, and to focus on what you want to do next and where you would like to do it.

The Computer—A Required Tool

The proliferation of increasingly sophisticated personal computers and the word processing and publishing software available for them have made PCs the personal tools of the 90s. In preparing a resume the PC is already more important than a pencil or a typewriter. You don't need to own one, but having access to one is essential. A PC accomplishes a great deal for you, so plan on using one for your resume preparation.

+ Alterations, revisions, changes, corrections
+ Content for content's sake
+ Variations on format
+ Economic advantages

= **Customer-Driven Resumes**

Personal Computers

1. A computer gives you the opportunity for endless alterations and corrections. Hopefully, this characteristic will not lead you to spend weeks attempting to create the perfect resume. Rather it will allow you to customize your resume to be customer-driven each time. We are not talking about misstatements of fact but we are talking about placing emphasis right where it belongs for each unique situation.

2. A computer allows you to concentrate on content when you need to, and concentrate on form when you need to. Immediate output, font selection, white space, content blocking—you can adjust all these as easily as a commercial printer can. Spell checkers and other tools within the software itself will warn you of misspelled and inappropriate

words and punctuation. But remember that these tools cannot substitute for a careful reading of every word on your resume. The last thing you want to do is blame the computer when your potential employer points out a mistake.

3. The personal computer and high-quality printers allow us to avoid the high cost that used to accompany any trip to the commercial printer for the mass printing of resumes. Now the only excuse you will have for not customizing the resume each time the situation warrants is yourself. With the targeted resume as your goal and a desktop or laptop computer by your side, you can quickly have an inventory of several versions of your resume stressing different aspects of your career and professional experiences. Now you can easily produce a tailored resume for each specific organization and job opening.

As important as the computer is, all your effort could be for naught if you don't use a letter-quality printer. Your resume and correspondence should not look like they were printed at home—they should all sparkle with professionalism. If your printer is not able to generate letter-quality work, investigate some of the computer usage locations in your area. Many provide economical use of their systems and have the most popular software available. You can bring in your disk with all your resume choices and correspondence, together with your own paper stock, and print on their laser printers very quickly.

Note: The personal computer may have been the tool of the 90s, but the information highway will be the tool of the rest of this and the next decade. Multimedia publishing, hypertext, and interactive websites are becoming the norm. (Just ask your children ... they are on-line and interactive either at school or at home.) Refer to Chapter 2 for further details about electronic resumes.

Summary

Resumes for Creative Jobs is a unique book because it warns every reader—regardless of profession—to pay constant attention to all aspects of the resume you are developing. Because a customer-driven, well-thought-out, attractive resume is now available to every applicant due to the proliferation of computers, you must rely on the fine points, the attention to detail and the creativity of your resume, to make it stand out. To remain competitive, you must have that professional edge honed to its sharpest.

While we encourage all job seekers to be creative in their resume preparation, this book is full of advice and warnings targeted specifically to those individuals seeking a job in a creative profession. Each person is encouraged to utilize his or her creativity by channeling it into the resume, because the resume serves as a first impression and calling card that should indicate the applicant is a creative thinker. Taking this road will not only make you a more effective applicant and generate more confidence in your abilities, skills, and aptitudes. It will also assist you professionally because it is one more avenue by which you can display to the world your unique ability to express yourself. That will help you set yourself apart from all the rest.

1

The Basics of Resume Writing

Even though it is not the good, or even the great, resumes that get you the job, a *targeted* resume can get you the interview that can get you the job! The key word is targeted; *the resume should be a match for the job you are applying for.* It should be geared to your audience. Will it be read by a human resources manager, department manager, division head, or personnel secretary? These are all gatekeepers who will review your resume. You must get past these gatekeepers to get to the individual who makes the hiring decision. Your resume is your passport. If you are the product, then the resume you send is the packaging. Your resume must sell **you**, and it must be a **you** that fits the job opening. See Fig. 1-1.

What Is a Resume?

A resume is a document that you should spend hours thinking about before you write even one word. It is the product of your best effort to reconstruct the past in the most positive light. You'll spend hours of your time writing a resume in the hope that someone with the power to hire you will spend 30 seconds reading it.

A resume is not your life history—not even a shortened version of it. A resume is a written response to the questions "Why should I want to interview you? What can you do for me?" A great interview can get you the job, but a great resume can get you that all-important interview—the critical step in the job search process.

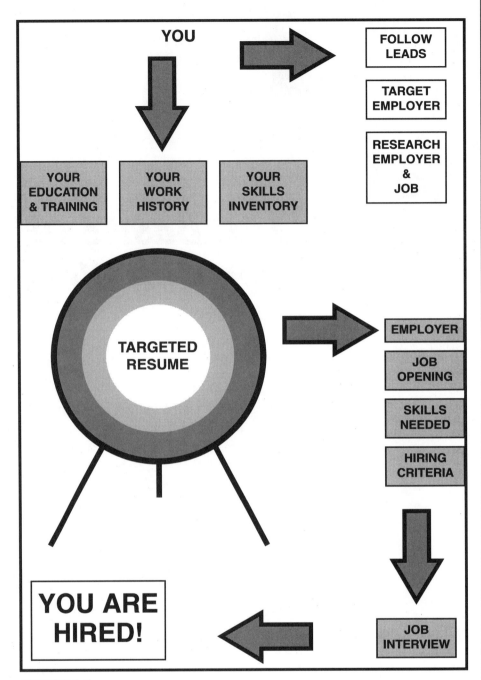

YOU

FOLLOW LEADS

TARGET EMPLOYER

RESEARCH EMPLOYER & JOB

YOUR EDUCATION & TRAINING

YOUR WORK HISTORY

YOUR SKILLS INVENTORY

TARGETED RESUME

EMPLOYER

JOB OPENING

SKILLS NEEDED

HIRING CRITERIA

JOB INTERVIEW

YOU ARE HIRED!

FIGURE 1-1.

Why Send Resumes?

Simply, you send resumes to sell yourself: to sell your skills, your talents, and your experiences. *Resumes are marketing tools; you are the product.* You are selling yourself as a solution to an organization's problem. The only way you can truly sell yourself is face to face, and the way to get invited to an interview is to submit a resume. Consider it a "sample," a preview of your entire sales pitch. A good resume answers the following questions posed by the reader:

1. What skills can you bring to our organization?
2. Are you going to be worth your salary?
3. Why should we interview you rather than all the other candidates?
4. How will you solve our problems?

Finally, the most persuasive reason for sending a resume is that *most employers want a resume.* Employers are not interested in oral histories or in wading through long letters. They want the facts, presented in a concise, professional, recognizable form. If it is visually exciting, creative, or a good read, then it will generate interest and cause the reader to take action—namely, to reach out and invite you to an interview.

If You Have a Resume, Do You Need a New One?

Review your most recent resume. If your resume is more than one year old (or for whatever reason appears old), you need a new one. You have learned new skills and increased your experience in a year's time; reflect these changes in your resume. Even if your resume still appears current, if you have been using versions of it with no results, now is the time to try a different tack. If it isn't working, fix it.

Before You Write One Word ... What Do You Want?

Yes, I know what you want—a job. But what type of job? Full-time, part-time, freelance? In a large organization or a small one? Do you want to work for a local company or are you willing to relocate? What is your goal?

To help you focus on some of your preferences, complete the following statements:

I would like to have a job doing:

_____

_____

_____

13

My responsibilities would include:

_____

_____

_____

This is the kind of organization I would like to work for:

_____

_____

_____

I am/am not willing to relocate.

My salary goal is (range)

$_____ .

I need the following benefits (medical, educational, child care, and so on):

_____

_____

You Have Taken the First Step

Focusing in on your job goal(s) is the first step in writing a winning resume. You may not have a specific job or organization in mind, but you certainly need a direction to go in. It is essential to know who you will be selling to. You may send resumes to organizations that you hear have job openings in your area, or to a specific company that you know has a vacancy that could fit you to a T. In either case, knowing who you are targeting will help you sell yourself in your resume more effectively.

The second step is to concentrate on what your product is. Consider the following questions:

What is it that you are selling?

What makes you different (better) than all the other applicants?

Are you selling the wide range of your abilities?

Are you selling your deep knowledge and experience in a specific area?

What direction are you going to lead the reader of your resume in?

Does your "product" match the needs of the prospective employer?

Can you paint a picture in the reader's mind of you in the job?

What You Say

Most of the resume writing takes place first in your mind. What should you put in the resume? Enough information to sell yourself. How long should a resume be? Usually, one or two pages for most positions. It should be *long enough to include all the pertinent information* but *concise enough not to lose or bore the reader.* A good resume should be short enough to give the employer a quick picture yet long enough to be convincing. You convince the reader by providing proof of your qualifications, by citing achievements, accomplishments, abilities, and skills. You get the employer to read this proof by presenting the information in an inviting way.

You Are in Control of What You Put into a Resume

Within your resume, you control disclosure. Of course, you will never falsify work or education experiences, but that does not mean you have to include everything in a resume. You may be asked for all the details on an application or in an interview, but in a resume you are in charge of putting yourself in the best light. Suppose you tried working in another city for two months and it didn't work out. Unless it serves a positive purpose, you do not have to include this information. What if you can type 120 wpm but do not ever want to work as a secretary, no matter what? Choose not to include that skill in your resume. If some areas are weak, such as Education, make that the last section and include recent course work or substitute "Professional Affiliations."

A Perfect Format

Even though no two resumes are the same, there are similarities of style and approach. Employers like to see resumes because they are easy to read and there are just so many formats they can be in. Additionally, because of the design of the resume itself, sections are clearly delineated that make some Yes–No decisions easy.

There is no one perfect resume format; each type organizes information in a different way. The key to any resume, regardless of format, is to present information in an easy-to-follow manner using concise statements. Lead from your strengths: What is your biggest selling point? Since what you decide to emphasize may differ depending on the job opening, you may want more than one resume in your arsenal. Each of the resume formats has advantages and disadvantages, as summarized in Fig. 1-2. We discuss each type in turn in the following section.

	ADVANTAGES	DISADVANTAGES
CHRONOLOGICAL RESUME	◆ Highlights strong work history ◆ Popular with traditional employers ◆ Positions you for the next move up the job ladder	◆ Reveals gaps in employment ◆ Employer has to search for relevant skills/experiences ◆ Can reveal your age ◆ Might show you've peaked—been in one job too long
FUNCTIONAL RESUME	◆ Focuses on current skills, not prior jobs ◆ Customer-driven ◆ Useful for job changers or those with interrupted work history ◆ Uses unpaid/volunteer work to your advantage ◆ Omits/plays down jobs that do not support your current goals	◆ Can be too narrow in approach ◆ Relies on candidate's insight into skills needed for job ◆ Does not allow for job progression record, if one exists ◆ May not reveal a clear job path
COMBINATION CHRONOLOGICAL/ FUNCTIONAL RESUME	◆ Can highlight skills not apparent in job history ◆ Stresses abilities germane to job opening ◆ Positive presentation of disjointed work history	◆ Cannot match skills with jobs ◆ May not show a clear career path ◆ Could underemphasize work experience ◆ Current goals not explained by work history
ALTERNATIVE RESUMES	◆ Industry norm is to include photo, graphics ◆ Innovative format highlights your creativity	◆ Unless done well, can look amateurish ◆ Can be perceived as a gimmick ◆ Turn-off for some conservative employers

FIGURE 1-2. **Types of Resumes**

Types of Resumes

1. Chronological Resume (Fig. 1-3)

This is the traditional resume format, listing in *reverse chronological order* your work and educational history. In many areas of employment, the chronological resume is the resume of choice. However, for individuals in many of the creative professions in which a patchwork of employers and experiences is the norm, this type of resume might not showcase their skills and talents to the best advantage. On the other hand, if the best thing that you have going for you at the moment is your association with a "name" organization or individual, a chronological format will draw attention to this fact. Some employers know that certain other companies or individuals foster talent; consequently, they are always eager to interview exiting employees from those firms.

An additional problem with a chronological resume is that it focuses on what you have done for other employers, while the prospective employer is thinking "What can he or she do for me now?" Also consider the fact that the employer may be faced with hundreds of resumes, each detailing 10, 15, or 25 years of work history. Visually, a listing of jobs may not be the most inspiring reading, and your resume must be inviting to read. Using a more suitable resume format may allow yours to stand out. Many employers in creative fields pride themselves as mavericks, and will appreciate the thought and care you put into making your resume unique.

2. Functional Resume (Fig. 1-4)

A functional resume (also called a targeted or focused resume) presents your skills and abilities in such a way as to make a strong candidate for a particular job. In professions in which a job history may involve frequent job changes or gaps in time, a functional resume may be more appropriate. For this format to be effective, you must have insight into the job requirements of the position for which you are applying, as well as the background to meet those requirements. Even if you are applying for a generic job opening, rather than a specific vacancy at Organization X, this format can be effective because it points the reader in a specific direction.

The main thrust of this type of resume should be "This is what I can do for you." By citing a specific job, you are saying

Name
Address
City, State Zip
Telephone Fax
E-mail

Objective: Refer to specific job/position

Summary: Statement of candidate's qualifications related to
                        specific job opening/position

**Professional Experience
and Accomplishments:**

Date 19xx-present   **Organization ABC**   City, State
                        Title/Position
                        Description/listing of prime responsibilities
                        highlighting those germane to current job
                        opening & organization
                        *Key accomplishments

Date 19xx-19xx   **Organization ABC**   City, State
                        Title/Position
                        Short description of prime responsibilities
                        *Key accomplishments

Date 19xx-19xx   **Organization ABC**   City, State
                        Title/Position
                        Short description of prime responsibilities
                        *Key accomplishments

**Education and
Professional Training:**

                        College/University/Trade School   City, State
                        Degree received
                        Seminars/workshops attended

**Professional
Awards:**   List citations, awards if appropriate

Affiliations: Professional memberships/activities

FIGURE 1-3. **Chronological Resume Format**

Name
Address
City, State Zip
Telephone Fax
E-mail

Objective: Refer to specific job/position; cite your qualifications/ accomplishments that support your candidacy. Use quantitative data (# years of experience, proficiencies, value added)

Competency:
(Top Skill #1)

Descriptive statement of transferable and learned skills obtained through work experiences
- Accomplishments, quantified if possible

Competency:
(Top Skill #2)

Descriptive statement of transferable and learned skills obtained through work experiences
- Accomplishments, quantified if possible

Competency:
(Top Skill #3,
Optional)

Descriptive statement of transferable and learned skills obtained through work experiences
- Accomplishments, quantified if possible

**Additional/Unique
Proficiencies:**   Related to job goal

Employment History:

Date 19xx-present	**Organization ABC** Job Title	City, State
Date 19xx-19xx	**Organization ABC** Job Title	City, State
Date 19xx-19xx	**Organization ABC** Job Title	City, State

Education: **College/University/Trade School**
City, State
Degree received

Seminars/workshops attended

**Professional
Awards:**   List citations, awards if appropriate

Affiliations: Professional memberships/activities

FIGURE 1-4. Functional Resume Format

"I can fill this job effectively." This is not the time to be vague; in your objective do not say "I want a job where I can use my skills effectively" and expect the reader to search for what those skills are. Be dynamic and precise:

> *"Position as a _____ (functional job title) using my ____(#) years of experience in _____ (doing related activities) with skills _____ (essential and unique to position)."*

State what you want and why you should get it. The body of your resume then supports your qualifications through your work history and accomplishments; you prove your claim to the job by means of your competencies. The key to this format is your identifying the skills and competencies essential to the position and presenting yourself as the candidate with just those skills.

3. Combination Chronological/Functional Resume (Fig. 1-5)

The combination resume hedges all bets by focusing on skills and achievements but still including a chronological listing of work and education histories. In many "creative" fields, education is the least important element, downplayed in favor of what you have done (and who you have done it with). If you have a work history related to the field in which you seek employment, provide details. If you have a history of jobs in and out of the profession, you may choose to list only those in the "business." This format will allow you to tie together different jobs by showing similarities of experience or growth.

4. Alternative Resume Formats

Special jobs have special needs. A banker would not (or should not) consider including personal characteristics such as height or hair color in a resume; an architect or photographer would not include a self-photograph but might include photos of past work. A model, dancer, performer, or actor is expected to submit glossies—black and white photos—in addition to personal characteristics including hair and eye color, height, and weight. Likewise, a singer, comedian, or musician would include a self-portrait because part of the product that is being sold is the physical appearance of the applicant. A graphic artist might enhance the resume itself with bold design elements, a creative format, or work samples.

Name
Address
City, State Zip
Telephone Fax
E-mail

Objective: Refer to specific job/position

Summary: Statement of candidate's qualifications related to spe-
                       cific job opening/position; provide details/quantita-
                       tive facts. Cite achievements, traits, proficiencies that
                       support your candidacy
                       • Summary of technical, equipment, technological
                       skills if appropriate

Competency: **Job Title, Proficiencies used**   Employer, Location
                       Descriptive statement of transferable and learned
                       skills obtained through work experiences
                       • Accomplishments, quantified if possible

Competency: **Job Title, Proficiencies used**   Employer, Location
                       Descriptive statement of transferable and learned
                       skills obtained through work experiences
                       • Accomplishments, quantified if possible

Competency: **Job Title, Proficiencies used**   Employer, Location
                       Descriptive statement of transferable and learned
                       skills obtained through work experiences
                       • Accomplishments, quantified if possible

Professional   College/University/Trade School   City, State
Training and**   Degree received
Education:
                       Seminars/workshops attended

**Professional
Awards:**   List citations, awards if appropriate

Affiliations: Professional memberships/activities

FIGURE 1-5. Combined Resume Format

The form of the alternative resume itself may differ: A three-fold pamphlet, press release, letter, or biographical sketch are all possibilities. If your resume extends to two pages, you could print it on 11 × 17 paper, folded in half. This particular booklet format could include the header and Objective or Summary on the cover, with the rest of the information inside, eliminating the risk of an employer's losing one page. One applicant very suitably submitted a cartoon strip outlining his artistic abilities. These types of resumes are used selectively when they are appropriate to a particular industry or position. When using these more imaginative approaches, it's important to remember to direct them to suitable employers and to be sure the resumes look professional. Additional details are provided in Chapter 2.

What Should Go into a Resume

No matter which format you use, you must have the facts at hand, as outlined in Fig. 1-6. Dates, places, who you worked with, what you did, why you made those choices, what you liked (and didn't like) about your prior jobs, all are fodder for an interview and the background for a strong resume. Since getting to the interview is the reason you are going through the resume exercise, get all your information together now. Writing, and periodically updating, your resume is an exercise in self-evaluation and planning for the future. While you are looking at and writing down what you have done, do it with an eye toward the future. If you see that there are gaps in your education or training, now is the time to work on filling them in by taking a class, joining a professional association, or learning a new skill.

Parts of a Resume

Objective

If you know the job you are applying for, then state it simply and clearly without rhetoric. For example, *Concierge for a large, metropolitan hotel. Experienced in all phases of public relations and customer service. Willing to relocate.* Or, *Creative animation position in both print and electronic media environments; experienced in pen & ink, color & background.* As mentioned earlier, don't be coy or go on a fishing expedition (*Looking for a position to use my skills*), leaving it up to the reader to determine exactly what it is you want. If you do not have a specific job in

Include:	Exclude:
Personal Data: Name, complete address, telephone number(s), fax number, e-mail address, website.	Data Too Personal: Birthdate/age, nicknames, marital situation, citizen status, spousal information, children's data.
Job Objective or Summary: Focus on prior experience or current job opening.	Scattershot approach: Vague statement on "using my skills" or "furthering my experience."
Work Experience: Correct and complete organization names, locations, job titles, dates (years), paid or unpaid internships.	Names[1] or telephone numbers of supervisors. Extensive details of jobs unrelated to current job goals, or too far in the past to be meaningful.
Educational History: Recent graduate (within past 5 years) may include GPA if exemplary; details of courses taken if related to job goals. Degree, major & minor if job-related. Training courses taken if related to current goals.	After 5 years, details of instructors, grades, or classes taken. Courses or training unrelated to job goals. Extracurricular activities (after 5 years). Incomplete courses or training programs.
Professional memberships and affiliations, current or within last 5 years. Offices held.	Political or religious activities.
Honors and awards, especially if job-related. No dates if older than 5 years.	Racial or ethnic "hints" or photos.[2]
Offer videos, audio tapes, samples of work or portfolios,[3] websites, magazine articles when available and appropriate.	Reference names and addresses. Comment "References available upon request."
Special interests or skills that highlight your other abilities (team player, competitive, varied interests).	Unrelated interests or skills; interests that could impact negatively, e.g., mountain climber—loner? risky? time off work?

[1]Include names of recognized experts or talent you have been associated with to show you have had excellent training.
[2]Exceptions are those professions in performing arts or modeling where personal appearance is an essential part of the application process.
[3]Portfolios, tapes, CDs, or work samples must also be prepared in a professional manner, be of excellent quality, and represent work that matches the targeted organization and job opening.

FIGURE 1-6. What to Put in Your Resume

mind or are not certain what jobs are open, omit the Objective; you could limit your choices by being unnecessarily specific.

If you have a greatly diversified background or are a new graduate or career-changer, you should definitely include a Job Objective or combine it with the Summary. An Objective should always be customized for the specific position you are applying for. The more targeted the Objective, the more effective it will be. The key purpose of any objective statement should be to spur the reader to read on.

Summary

A summary may be used with or instead of an Objective. In a functional resume, the Summary refers to previous jobs and experiences. For example, *Proven effective Art Department Coordinator with 3 years' experience. Computer literate. Team-based manager.* In a combined resume, the Summary should highlight the skills that apply to the prospective job. Avoid fluff: *Energetic go-getter, hands-on,* and similar phrases have been used so often they are meaningless even if they are true. Show the employer that you are energetic by citing specific accomplishments (*increased market share 20%, designed new packaging that cut shipping expenses 12%*).

As with an Objective, the more the summary statement is related to the job you are applying for, the more effective it will be. If you have a tough time deciding whether to use a Summary or an Objective at the top of your resume, use this general rule to help you decide: The more experience you have, the more you should lean toward a Summary; the less relevant experience (if you are changing or starting a career), the more effective an Objective will be. The primary purpose of this section is to set the reader up for your proof of qualifications, skills, experience, or training; you want to point the employer in the right direction.

Employment or Work History

Information as to dates, places, supervisors, salary rates, and reasons for leaving will certainly come up either on an application form or at an interview. If you have already gathered all this information, you have gotten together a winning resume while also preparing yourself for an interview! Use the Work History Worksheet (Fig. 1-7) to keep all your facts straight. When writing the resume, consider a bulleted approach to highlight accomplishments, to avoid a block of text. For example:

⊃ Created 6 major advertising campaigns in past 18 months.

⊃ Developed POP displays that enabled client to increase sales 3%.

⊃ Trained staff of 5 on CAD programs.

Note to Job-Hoppers Some industries or professions see employees with very scattered work histories as an industry standard (and perhaps even consider the opposite odd). If this pertains to you, show continuity of employment in a particular line of work or competencies. For example, a stage manager may have worked for ten different organizations during the last five years (given the project nature and uncertain financial vagaries of the theater); showing recurring employment in the field is essential, as in Fig. 1-8.

List, in reverse chronological order, all full- and part-time employment and supporting details.
Organization: Address & phone #: Supervisor name & title: Dates of employment: Your title: Job description: Key responsibilities: Skills used/learned: Projects/assignments: Comments: Beg. Salary: $ Ending Salary: $
Organization: Address & phone #: Supervisor name & title: Dates of employment: Your title: Job description: Key responsibilities: Skills used/learned: Projects/assignments: Comments: Beg. Salary: $ Ending Salary: $
Organization: Address & phone #: Supervisor name & title: Dates of employment: Your title: $ Job description: Key responsibilities: Skills used/learned: Projects/assignments: Comments: Beg. Salary: $ Ending Salary: $

FIGURE 1-7. **Work History Worksheet**

Pat Jones
77 Boxer Street
New York, New York 10012
212-477-1234 Fax 212-477-1235
E-Mail pjones@jones.com

Summary: Award-winning radio program director with over 7 years' experience seeking to make sweet music with a radio station wishing to be on cutting edge of music

Professional Highlights:

1995 MusArt Program Director of the Year
1989 & 1993 Dever Award "Most Creative Program Director"

Program Director:

RSTU Radio　　　　　New York, NY　　　1995-1996
- Initiated "Talk is Cheap," rated #1 talk show NYC
- "Noon Music" show moved up from #11 to #3 in first 6 months of programming

(Station sold to C1City; format changing to all news)

WEST Radio　　　　　Denver, CO　　　1994-1995
- Initiated "New Wave" talk show; captured 15% market share after 9 months of programming
- Created programming team to bring new western music to airwaves; voted #1 station June, 1995

(Recruited by NYC station)

KLDG Radio　　　　　Silver, CO　　　1992-1995
- DJ at college station; promoted to assistant program manager senior year.
- Introduced "Music Talk," voted most creative new show

Disc Jockey: BKSS Radio　Copper, CO　　1989-1992
- JazzRock format; interviews with performers

Education: Wiltshire University　Copper, CO　　BA 1992

FIGURE 1-8. **Job-Hopper Resume Sample**

Note to Job-Keepers Even though there is still some respect for personal loyalty to organizations, show through your experiences that even though you stayed in one or two organizations for a long period of time, you grew on the job through increasingly challenging assignments. Treat individual assignments as you would if you were a job-hopper who had joined several organizations. Include names of divisions or subsidiaries to enhance that image.

Education

Unless you have just recently graduated (less than five years ago), this area will be fairly straightforward and concise. For example,

Education   B.A. in English, magna cum laude, Harvard College, Cambridge, Massachusetts. Phi Beta Kappa. (*Date is optional.*)

Employers will be more interested in what you have done than in what you have studied. If you have had on-the-job training, rather than a traditional classroom experience, this is the area to highlight your knowledge. Many skills, such as videotape editing, may be taught in a classroom, but are really learned by working with professionals in the "real world."

On the Education Worksheet (Fig. 1-9), list your educational background in most recent order, including classes, seminars, workshops, apprenticeships, internships, and volunteer work as they pertain to your field. If a key part of your background is that you studied with or were involved in a hands-on learning experience with an acknowledged expert, this is the place to cite those credentials. Learning to cook at a local community college's adult education program is one type of experience; doing so when the instructor is a famous chef is another. Give yourself credit for associating yourself with talent, no matter where you have found it.

Note to Recent Graduates You should stress the content of studies that pertain to your job search; if you studied under any notable experts, also cite them in your resume but remember to select only job-relevant topics. Since you may not have an extensive work history to offer, you should go into more detail regarding professional courses that you have taken, as in the sample resume (Fig. 1-11) taking Pat Jones back a few years.

Using the chart below, list your educational background, in reverse chronological order. Do not neglect workshops or seminars attended. Detail next to each entry those skills or accomplishments that you can bring to the job.

DATES	SCHOOLS, SEMINARS, WORKSHOPS, PRESENTATIONS	RELATED JOB SKILLS LEARNED

FIGURE 1-9. Education Worksheet

Pat Jones

77 Boxer Street   212-477-1234   Fax 212-477-1235
New York, New York 10012   E-Mail pjones@jones.com

SUMMARY

Video editor with 4 years' experience, VHS, Beta, 16mm and 8mm formats. Assistant editor for *"Wonderful World of Dance"* (R. C. Graves, editor); Emmy Award for video editing, 1994.

EXPERIENCE

"From the Grave" Productions   *New York City*

1995-96

§   Edited 17 segments of *"Inside Out"* drama series for WDGT-TV (series cancelled by network due to casting problems)

1994

§   Assistant editor with R. C. Graves on Emmy-nominated show *"Wonderful World of Dance"* for EBS.

Video 2000   *New York City*

1992-94

§   Assistant video editor responsible for all public television shows; on-line and off-line editing.

1989-92

§   Mail room supervisor; computerized delivery system, which resulted in 25% faster turn-around time on videos delivered. Loss record reduced 13% due to tracking system.

EDUCATION

Hirsch Film School   *New York City*   *BA, 1992*

§   Graduated "Summa cum laude"

§   Edited student film *"Park Squirrels,"* winner of LAUREL PRIZE, 1992

FIGURE 1-10.

Pat Jones
77 Boxer Street
New York, New York 10012
212-477-1234 Fax 212-477-1235
E-Mail pjones@jones.com

Objective: Newspaper production assistant utilizing 3 years' on-the-job training; willing to relocate.

Skills: 2 years' experience with Quark XPress, Adobe Photo-Shop, PageMaker and Illustrator; able to do mechanicals and paste-ups. Pre-production experience.

Experience: **CTPress** **Oxford, NY** **1993-1996**
Production assistant at weekly newspaper responsible for designing clients' ads and preparing boards for print. Handled client base of over 50 accounts.
• Upgraded press' computer software; Windows95/NT. Trained staff of 12 on network.

Intern — Production assistant **1992-1993**
• Work-study program affiliated with Barton College. Assisted in design and production of client ads; liaised with print department.

Education: **Barton College** **Oxford, NY** **BA, 1995**
Teaching Assistant: Communications, Prof. D. Edmunds, 1996-present

Editor: **"Barton Bugle"** **1994-1995**
Responsible for producing monthly campus newsletter; designed layout and prepared ads on MS Publisher.

Production Manager: **1996 Barton Yearbook**

Seminars: **Microsoft Print, Jan. 1996**
Washington, DC

FIGURE 1-11. Recent Graduate Resume Sample

Affiliations/Professional Memberships

If you are active in your profession, state how, where, and in what capacity. The affiliations you include should mirror your professional status at an appropriate level and reflect your approach to your career. Names of professional associations should be totally accurate. Acronyms should be avoided. Consider the following example:

Professional Memberships   **American Society of Interior Designers**
Societe de Fabrique

Awards/Citations/Honors

If you or your work have been recognized or awarded, give details. You may consider omitting this section if it has been a number of years since the recognition was received, to avoid the "What has he or she done lately?" syndrome. Eliminating time-sensitive references (for example, dates) may be a way to skirt the question. See the example below:

Awards   Received several grants from the New York State Council on the Arts for original projects in theater.

Special Skills

Special skills should be included if they are not identified anywhere else in the resume and merit special attention. Determine whether the skills you wish to mention are a resume enhancement. Whether you consider your kazoo playing of real value should be reviewed in light of the position you are applying for. That talent may be of real interest to a kazoo manufacturer, but may do less than nothing for your prospects in a lot of other organizations (unless, of course, one of the gatekeepers there shares the same interest). In any event, always consider carefully whether what you wish to include in this category will help you get your foot in the door or serve to keep you out. For instance, a global leader in sports entertainment that we know of tends to be conservative about considering fans for employment because of the influence that might have on their job performance.

On the other hand, there are job-related skills that should be mentioned. Consider the following resume excerpts:

Special Skills   **3rd Degree Black Belt, Aikido; drumming; dialects; stage fighting.**

and

Special Skills   Fluent in French and Italian
Carpentry and framing

References/Work Samples

Of course, if you are interviewed and you are asked for references you will supply them. So why take up valuable space in your resume to state the obvious? However, if you are an artist, photographer, filmmaker, or other professional with a portfolio or work samples, state that your portfolio, book, or tape is available upon request. For example:

Complete Portfolio Available Upon Request

How Many Resumes Do You Need?

Sending mass mailings of your standard, one-size-fits-all resume may make you feel like you are doing something to get a job, but the truth of the matter is that nearly 80 percent of jobs come from leads or referrals that you develop. Spread the word: Let everyone know you are searching for a job and that you could really use their help. You never know—someone you may least suspect may have a contact in the business. Cast your net wide unless you are currently employed and shopping around, in which case discretion is the better attitude to adopt.

Even if you are unable to be working in your chosen profession, keep active in it by attending seminars, reading publi-

- Parents/grandparents
- Other blood relatives
- Distant relatives
- In-laws
- Former in-laws
- Church or synagogue members
- Your (or a neighbor's) children's sports league and other school activity contacts
- School contacts
- Newspaper vendor
- Video store owner
- Other shop contacts
- Gas station/auto repair shop owners
- Co-op/condominium board members/contacts
- Political contacts
- School contacts and acquaintances
- Alumni directory
- Placement Office
- Caterers
- Tailor
- Friends/contacts of relatives
- Fellow customers

FIGURE 1-12. Potential Sources/Network Opportunities

cations, or going to professional meetings. Keeping active in your profession even when you are not directly employed will keep your mind active, can keep you up on all the latest events and developments, will help you build professional contacts, and will keep you "out there" in the field. You never know who may prove helpful to your job search. See Fig. 1-12 for further suggestions on getting job leads.

Picking a Target

The benefit of following leads is that it allows you to research your target employer.

What exactly does this organization do?

How do they make money?

How has business been lately?

What kind of people work there?

Who will I send the resume to?

Is this person in HR or in a line position?

Will this person make the hiring decision or is he or she a gatekeeper?

Knowing your target will allow you to focus your resume. The single most important aspect of a resume today is that it be customer-driven, to the greatest extent possible.

Sending Your Resume to the Right Place

Selecting the organization to send your resume to is a major decision and may be similar to finding a needle in a haystack. Just for starters, take note of the fact that in the private sector alone, there are more than eleven million businesses in existence throughout the United States at any moment, according to the U.S. Chamber of Commerce.

Are you looking for full-time or part-time employment? A recent article in the *Wall Street Journal* referred to "casserole" careers, describing a growing trend of individuals building more than one career. A dancer may get involved in costuming, staging, or choreography. A chef may write a cookbook or a food column in a local newspaper. In the old days (as recently as the early 80s), professionals (except for fast-track MBAs) were rated on their organizational loyalty, and the key determinant was the length of time a person stayed with his or her first organization. Two business books written in the mid-80s by Charles Handy (*The Age of Unreason*) and William Houze (*Career Veer*) stated that the old emphasis on loyalty was dead and professionals should be driven first by themselves in an ongoing effort to stay current and marketable. Handy went so far as to say that the successful professional of the future would be the one who had at least *three different careers* during one professional lifetime. So, if you have been job-hopping, consider yourself on the cutting edge!

A resume can also be used to find freelance work, either as a career choice or to tide you over until you have gained more experience or found the right position. Many freelancers, having found very lucrative and satisfying work in this venue, have moved into the role of entrepreneur; they are no longer interested in finding employers but are looking for clients instead. A chef could move into the catering business, using his or her resume as credentials to enlist business. If you prefer the organizational side of work and would prefer to be an employee, bear in mind that a freelance assignment often becomes permanent when an employer reaches a comfort level with the freelancer and determines at some point in time that there is sufficient business to cement the employer–employee relationship.

Who are your targets? Who are you selling yourself to? Complete the Target Profile (Fig. 1-13) to focus in on your target job.

Avoid Mass Mailings

Any resume you submit to any organization should link your skills and experiences to that organization, so that whoever screens your resume will see the profile of a real problem solver with potential value for that organization. You must position yourself as the solution to the employer's problems. To do that you must know what the position is, what the job requirements are, and what kind of person they are looking for to fill the position. Then, write a resume that solves their problem by stressing those aspects of your background that make you the ideal candidate. This method of targeting a resume is not possible with mass mailings.

If you are following up on a blind ad (and have no idea who the employer is), be certain to qualify yourself for the job by citing in your resume the requirements mentioned in the ad. If the ad states *"4 years' minimum experience in Quark*

List below all the information available about the industry, organization, and job opening you are applying for.

Industry: _____
Current trends/issues:

Organization: _____
Location(s):
Standing in the industry:
Current issues:

Profit/earnings picture:
Current growth phase:
Major service(s)/product(s):

Key executives:
Prime competition:

Job Opening/Position: _____
Title:
Responsibilities:

New position/vacant since:

Reporting to:
Staff size/work group:
Salary range:

FIGURE 1-13. **Target Profile**

XPress," be sure to show in the resume that you have it. These resumes will pass through a gatekeeper who will tick off a list of requirements before a resume can be passed on for further review. Your resume has to pass the gatekeeper's review for you to even be considered for an interview.

With the availability of computers in homes, public libraries, computer stores, or nationwide chains such as Kinko's, there is no need to limit yourself to one, all-purpose resume. If you are a graphic artist, you can have one resume highlighting your work done for magazines, and another pointing out your experiences in advertising, to send to the appropriate targeted employers. You need different approaches for different types of employers. If your experience has been in large organizations, with a customer-driven resume you can sell your wide range of experiences to a smaller firm; and you can play up the "just like you" aspects when applying to large organizations.

Marketing Yourself: Can You Do It? Will You? Will You Fit In?

It is not dates, places, or college backgrounds that most employers are looking for. The individual doing the hiring may have a hidden agenda in choosing particular types of applicants, but most organizations just want good hires who will do the job. Organizations want individuals who will add value to the organization. They are looking for "can do...will do...fit" candidates, competent individuals with transferable skills.

Can do = You have the required skills, training, abilities, and experiences to do the job.

Will do = You have the motivation; you have handled these types of responsibilities before and you have the drive to *want* to do them again. (That you will do it again will not be assumed by a potential employer.)

FIT = You will complement or provide needed balance to an existing work group or team. You will be a participant in the team. This is the soft aspect of assessment that grows in importance the higher up the organization you go. The technical skills and motivation are now assumed; the ingredient that will make or break a candidacy now is the ability of the applicant to be assimilated by the work group. The most skilled person with the greatest motivation will fail if that person is not accepted by the work group. For this reason author Harvey Mackay (*Eat with the Sharks or Be Eaten Alive*) says that in his company, he requires all applicants to go through twelve to fifteen interviews.

What Exactly Can You Do? What Is Your "Job"?

A film editor does not just sit at a machine all day. Organizational skills, teamwork skills, communication skills, and problem-solving skills, to name a few, are integral to that job and are used daily. Why not give yourself credit for all the skills that you can bring to the table? By recognizing all the hidden skills

List below, next to the various competencies, those skills you have to offer and provide brief details as to where/when you acquired these skills. Space is provided to add your own.

Competencies:	Specifics:	Where/when acquired:
Organization Planning, facilitating, motivating, prioritizing		
Communication Oral & written, nonverbal, feedback		
Management Decision making, supervising, mentoring, implementing, leading		
Finance Budgeting, reporting, planning, recording		
Problem solving Identifying, defining, evaluating, selecting		
Teamwork Team building, supporting, collaborating, developing, motivating		
Information Management Compile, rank, sort, synthesize, evaluate, utilize		
Research Investigate, explore sources, define problem, question, test solutions		
Interpersonal Goal-oriented, delegate, interact, commitment, teach, demonstrate		

FIGURE 1-14. Skills Inventory

needed to fulfill a job, you can convey to a prospective employer in your resume your complete understanding of the nature of the job. Virtually every job—from hair stylist to screenwriter—involves competencies far beyond the technical requirements for the job. What are yours? Take an inventory of all your skills; do not discount those that you may have not used for a year or two. Use the Skills Inventory (Fig. 1-14) to list yours.

The final element, fit, will be assayed in the interview. How well will you fit into the organization, the work group, the team? This is a very subjective part of the job application process but you can only sell yourself in person *if* you get the interview. Your resume is your one shot to get in the door for a face-to-face meeting. By acknowledging the importance of teams and interpersonal relationships and the dynamics of the work group in your resume, you will be conveying to the employer your understanding that they must hire individuals who fit in.

Now What? Write Your Resume

You have all the facts, so now write your resume. You are the expert on you: your education, your skills, your experience, your area of expertise, what you want in a job. Thanks to the research you have done on the organization, the industry, and the job opening, you can qualify as an expert in applying for the job you want.

What Should You Say? (Who Will Be Reading It?)

Remember, the resume should be customer-driven. Your resume has to meet some basic requirements to make the first cut. It has been said that at the most senior levels, the qualifications needed are the most specific in a soft sort of way (i.e., whole industries and organizations are included or excluded with a sweeping comment). Entry-level jobs, although limited in number, are specific in their hard requirements simply because skill demands are easier to define. It takes much longer, for instance, to determine the skill level of an executive producer than that of a videotape editor. Additionally, selection at the lower levels may be more precise for another reason: Employers can afford to be more selective due to the number of applicants trying out for those few, choice spots (consider, for example, the ability of employers to offer unpaid internships).

Between the senior levels and entry level are the many positions in the broad middle range.

This middle range is a prime area for resume effectiveness, because organizations have a wider spectrum in this area to define the best applicant. A multitude of skills and experiences in this expanse are both transferable and desired by many potential employers. If you offer the appropriate skills package in a resume to the right employer, you can increase your probability of being invited for an interview.

Summary

Resume writing is a discipline that requires patience and persistence. Getting it done is not enough, it must be done effectively. How to tell? Use your resume to get your foot in the door and you'll know it works. Use it to get hired and you'll know it was effective.

Nobel Prize-winning author Arno Penzias, in his recent book *Harmony: Business, Technology and Life after Paperwork,* stated that knowledge and its acquisition are in demand by more and more employers as the essential traits its workforce requires as change continues to dominate the marketplace. If knowledge is increasingly being sought by employers as the real value each employee brings to an organization, then more than ever the appeal of the creative professional seeking a job will be his or her ability to demonstrate to every potential employer, from the start, the knowledge he or she initially brings to the table. You can demonstrate this by developing a resume that on its very face indicates that you take no aspect of the job search process for granted.

---

1. **Take an inventory of yourself.** Complete the Work History, Education, and Skills Inventories.
2. **Establish job goals.** What type of work are you looking for: part-time, freelance to tide you over, or only full-time employment? What kind of employers and organizations are you considering? Have you explored alternatives? Have you done research on the job openings and organizations that you are targeting? Are you exploring job leads?
3. **Complete a first draft of your resume.** Choose a format that is appropriate to your particular work and educational history.
4. **Double check all your information.** Are all your facts straight? Names, dates, and locations must be accurate.

FIGURE 1-15. **Basics of Resume Writing**

Consider the resume in all its aspects as you draft it (see Fig. 1-15). Then compare it conceptually with the particular job you are applying for. Give it the critical glance of the person for whom it is intended. Look at the format to determine whether that enhances the content. Only then should you consider your resume ready to be submitted.

2

Writing It Right

Whether your resume will be processed manually or scanned (see the discussion of electronic resumes later in this chapter), your writing must be concise and dynamic. That is, you should portray yourself as someone who makes things happen. Do not describe things that happened; tell about what you did. Consider the action words in the following list (Fig. 2-1); how many did you apply to your background and use in your draft resume? Do not be passive. Paint yourself as a doer, an active participant. Revise your resume to use active words whenever possible; do not be afraid to use a thesaurus to find inspired variations on old standards such as "increased," "designed," and so forth.

Put Yourself in the Employer's Spot

What is the employer looking for? If the company suggests a work group atmosphere, tout your team player attitude. Will you have a staff? Are you a doer or a delegator? (Don't forget that many organizations eliminated the delegator positions in downsizing.) Credibility is gained by portraying yourself as an active, involved participant. Remember, too, that you will be more desirable if you are perceived as flexible. Demonstrate it by showing that you've worn more than one hat and have successfully handled multiple priorities and projects ... if you have.

Cite leadership (vs. management) as a skill. What essential elements would be included in the job description? Write your-

Circle all the action words that you can apply to yourself. How many can you legitimately use in your resume? Add your own.

Acquired	Directed	Oversaw	Tested
Administered	Distributed	Performed	Trained
Advised	Drew	Planned	Translated
Analyzed	Drew up	Prepared	Wrote
Arbitrated	Edited	Prescribed	_____
Arranged	Eliminated	Presented	_____
Assembled	Evaluated	Processed	_____
Assisted	Examined	Produced	_____
Audited	Expanded	Programmed	_____
Built	Formulated	Promoted	_____
Calculated	Identified	Protected	_____
Charted	Implemented	Provided	_____
Collected	Improved	Purchased	_____
Completed	Increased	Received	_____
Composed	Installed	Recorded	_____
Conducted	Instituted	Reduced	_____
Conserved	Instructed	Referred	_____
Constructed	Interpreted	Rendered	_____
Consulted	Interviewed	Researched	_____
Controlled	Invented	Restored	_____
Coordinated	Lectured	Reviewed	_____
Counseled	Logged	Rewarded	_____
Created	Managed	Routed	_____
Criticized	Navigated	Sang	_____
Delivered	Negotiated	Selected	_____
Designed	Networked	Served	_____
Detected	Observed	Sold	_____
Determined	Obtained	Solved	_____
Developed	Operated	Studied	_____
Devised	Ordered	Supervised	_____
Diagnosed	Organized	Supplied	_____

FIGURE 2-1. Action Words

self in by citing those elements meeting the needs of the job. What are the priorities of the job? List these as your top skills or relate them to your accomplishments. Notice that earlier the word "perceived" was used because what the reader will do in reading your resume is develop a perception of who you are, how you see yourself, and how you sell yourself as a potential member of the organization.

Lead from Strength

Once you have identified the most important elements of the job, be sure to sell those areas first in your resume. If being computer literate is the most essential element of the job and is one of your skills, lead off with your qualifications in that area. If you have worked with and trained under the best in your field, begin with either your employment or education history to spotlight those experiences.

Can you fit yourself into the picture? Match the job's requirements to the skills you listed previously (Fig. 1-14), and offer proof that you can do and will do. *This job demands creativity; I have created 23 innovative radio ads in the last 6 months.* Quantify whenever possible. Use the form in Fig. 2-2 to see if you have what is needed to sell yourself as a match for the job opening you have targeted.

List in the left column all of the skills, competencies, and technical requirements of the position for which you are applying in order of priority.
In the column on the right, insert an example from your work or education history of when you have used that skill. These are the areas to spotlight in your resume. Quantify when possible.

ORGANIZATION: _____

JOB TITLE: _____

JOB DESCRIPTION: _____

	THE JOB NEEDS ...	I HAVE ...
1		
2		
3		
4		
5		
6		
7		
8		
9		
10		

FIGURE 2-2. **Putting Yourself in the Picture**

Your Resume Is Out of Your Hands

How will you be sending your resume? There are choices to be made. How will it be handled? Who will read it?

The vast majority of resumes continue to be manually processed. Years ago this would just have been assumed. All resumes were read only by humans. Recently, computers with ever more sophisticated technology have become the screening process of choice for a growing number of organizations. Be prepared for both—have a resume prepared that will be effective whether it is read by humans or computers. (For electronic resume processing, see further details in this chapter.) Resumes can be e-mailed or faxed, posted on-line, or just mailed.

Fax Mail

Fax machines are subject to as many vagaries as scanners; some are excellent while others may skew or blur your text. When faxing a resume you will never go wrong if you follow these guidelines, which are useful for scanned resumes as well:

- Avoid using colored papers, elaborate graphics, or complicated typefaces.
- Try a test fax; send your resume to a friend by fax and then review the product.
- Do not fax a document that has ever been folded.

Welcome to the Nineties! Electronic or Scanned Resumes

A small (but growing) number of resumes are scanned. Many large organizations use electronic databases (ATS: Applicant Tracking Systems) to read resumes. Resumes are scanned into the computer database as text and then translated through OCR (optical character recognition) into a text file (ASCII). According to pre-set fields, information such as your name, address, telephone number, work history, years of experience, education, and skills is read from the scanned text. Usually the program searches for nouns or keywords. Depending on the software program used, the employer will store either your scanned resume or a condensed version of it in its computer database. If you are applying for a job in a large organization, call the Human Resources or Personnel department to ask if they scan resumes, as there are some special rules to follow when submitting a resume that you know will be scanned.

On-Line Resumes

The fastest-growing group of resumes is electronic resumes. The increase in newsgroups, bulletin boards (BBSs), and World Wide Web (WWW) sites on the Internet has expanded access to both job seekers and employers. Employers can either post their job openings on the Internet or search using search engines (special on-line applications that look for data, keywords, or concepts, such as Yahoo, Excite, or Internet Sleuth) in a multitude of sites for resumes that have been posted that meet their criteria. You can post your resume either electronically by e-mail or by uploading files, or by mailing a hard (paper) copy of the resume to the organization sponsoring the website. In most cases, posting of your resume is free or low-cost ($10.00 for a mailed copy to be posted). These sites are supported by payments from employers who want their jobs openings listed, recruiters who wish to search the database for resumes, and candidates who want to be included in databases.

Special Rules for Electronic Resumes

There are special rules for presentation of resumes that will be posted on the Internet or will be scanned by employers into an Applicant Tracking System (ATS). If you have called a targeted employer's Personnel or Human Resources department to inquire if they scan resumes and have learned that they do so, you can prepare a resume that is both readable and on target (thus placing you ahead of all the other unknowing applicants). The main differences in writing a resume for electronic reading are the use of keywords and the visual presentation.

If you want your resume to be literally picked out for certain jobs, you must include specific terms in your resume. Some electronic resumes include a section marked **Keywords** at the top to aid in the electronic reading of the resume. If you are applying for a position as a computer graphic artist, use the term "computer graphic artist" as well as listing all the programs and applications you are proficient in. You have to put yourself into the mind of the gatekeeper (which in this case is a computer program or a search engine), and put all the ingredients into your resume that can match its menu. For example, a chef might insert keywords such as "culinary arts," "cuisine," "caterer," or "cook."

Scanned Resumes

In addition to complying with all the requisites for a search by supplying keywords in an electronic resume, you must also consider the vagaries of scanners themselves.

- Scanners usually do not read fonts or typefaces with serifs, such as **Times Roman** or **Bookman Old Style** or `Courier`. Use a clear sans-serif font such as **Arial**.
- Leave out the FANCY LETTERHEAD or ☞ graphics. Use white space to set areas apart.
- **Do not** use colored paper.
- **Do not** fold your resume. Mail it flat in a 9 × 12 envelope.
- Use a good quality paper that can withstand machine feed and processing.
- **Do not** staple pages together.
- Use of **bold**, <u>underlining</u>, or *italics* will most likely be rejected by or confuse the scanner. Don't use them. If you wish to set off areas, use + (plus) or 0 (zero) instead of bullets.

Clearly, the *content* of these resumes is the focus because you cannot catch the computer's eye with fancy footwork in your presentation. However, even within these narrow confines, you can show your creativity in how you lay out your information on the page. Is it centered, flush left, broken up with captions or white spaces? Do not forget that even though a lowly computer may select your resume, it will be seen and judged by a human who will decide whether to interview you or not. See Pat Jones' resume redone for an employer with an ATS in Fig. 2-3.

Posting On-Line

The Internet is constantly changing and being updated continuously, so there is no absolute figure as to how many jobs are listed on the Internet on any given day. Posting your resume on a bulletin board or newsgroup is akin to hanging up a copy of your resume at the grocery store; it will be seen by some people, but will the right people see it? Will the people with the right jobs and the power to hire you see it?

There is no security on the Internet, so if you post your resume you cannot control who will see it. Alternatively, you can respond to job postings by e-mailing or faxing your resume directly to a prospective employer. If you have access to the Internet, you can search the Web via search engines such as Yahoo, Excite, Magellan, or AltaVista, to name but a few. There are numerous books explaining the Internet and if you wish to get your toes wet now, this is a good chance to learn a new skill.

Pat Jones
77 Boxer Street
New York, New York 10012
212-477-1234   Fax 212-477-1235
E-Mail pjones@jones.com

KEYWORDS: Production Assistant, 3 years' newspaper experience, college graduate, Quark XPress, Adobe PhotoShop, PageMaker, Illustrator, MSPublisher, Windows95/NT, mechanicals, board work, pre-production experience

OBJECTIVE: Newspaper production assistant utilizing 3 years' on-the-job training; willing to relocate.

SKILLS: 2 years' experience with QuarkXPress, Adobe PhotoShop, PageMaker and Illustrator; able to do mechanicals and paste-ups. Pre-production experience.

EXPERIENCE: CTPress   Oxford, NY   1993-1996
Production assistant at weekly newspaper responsible for designing clients' ads and preparing boards for print. Handled client base of over 50 accounts. Upgraded press' computer software; Windows95/NT. Initiated training of 5 member staff on network.

Intern — Production Assistant   1992-1993
Work-study program affiliated with Barton College. Assisted in design and production of client ads; liaised with print department.

EDUCATION: Barton College   Oxford, NY   BA, 1995
Teaching Assistant: Communications, Prof. D. Edmunds, 1996-present.

Editor: "Barton Bugle"   1994-1995
Responsible for producing monthly campus newsletter; designed layout and prepared ads on MSPublisher.

Production Manager: 1996 Barton Yearbook

Seminars: Microsoft Print, Jan. 1996

FIGURE 2-3. **Sample Scanned Resume**

Web Basics

World Wide Web (WWW) sites, such as *Career Mosaic* or *Career Magazine,* provide resources for both job seekers and employers. Postings of resumes on the Internet have grown astronomically in recent years. *Career Web* reports listings of more than 4,000 resumes as of July 1996 and over 500 jobs listed. Gary Resnikoff, President of *Career Magazine,* a web site, stated that *"Career Magazine* has about 400,000+ job listings ... and about 75,000 resumes downloaded per month." You can access a site directly by typing in its URL (uniform resource locator) address.

Additionally, there are newsgroups (Usenet discussion groups) where anyone can post a job, an inquiry, or a resume. Newsgroups can be organized geographically (U.S., Atlanta, Pennsylvania), by industry (computers, media), or topically (music, professional wrestling, children's books). Some of the topics can challenge your understanding and one never knows if the topic is being adhered to or not. The best advice is to "lurk" for awhile—read the postings and follow the discussion before posting your resume to see if the group is for you.

According to Gary Resnikoff, there are approximately 7,000 to 8,000 resumes entered into resume newsgroups each week with another 5,000 to 7,000 jobs posted to the jobs newsgroups daily. There are more than 15,000 newsgroups, and access to them is dependent upon your Internet Service Provider (ISP).

On-Line Resources

To use search sites (Internet Sleuth) or search engines (Yahoo, Magellan) to access job listings, you must use keywords such as "resume," "jobs," "career," "employment," or whatever specific career field you are in, e.g., "calligrapher." Some sites or search engines organize information into topics (entertainment, government, career, shopping). You will be provided with a list of hot links to click on that will lead you to further information or to other lists or websites.

For example, if you did a search for keyword "resume," you would be provided with a list of hosts with websites that relate to resumes. You may also find sites titled *"My Resume,"* or *"Here's the Wonderful Resume of ____,"* or *"Resume, resume, resume ..."* repeated 20 times (indicating the posting of someone who heard about keywords a few too many times). Some general sites that you may want to investigate are listed in Fig. 2-4. Many offer free posting of resumes.

WORLD WIDE WEB SITES

- Career Mosaic   http://www.careermosaic.com
- The Monster Board   http://www.monster.com.80
- IntelliMatch   http://www.intellimatch.com
- Career Magazine   http://www.careermag.com
- Career Web   http://www.cweb.com
- Internet Job Locator   http://www.joblocator.com/jobs/
- Career Path   http://www.careerpath.com
- Shawn's Internet
  Resume Center   http://www.inpursuit.com
- E-Span   http://www.espan.cim
- Online Career Center   http://www.occ.com/occ
- Job Trak   http://www.jobtrak.com
- Eagle View   http://www.eagleview.com

NEWSGROUPS

- us.jobs.resumes   • misc.jobs.resumes

Also available by cities, states, and foreign countries. Look also for newsgroups specializing in your field: arts, media, computers, theater.

SEARCH ENGINES

- Yahoo   http://www.yahoo.com
- Magellan   http://www.mckinley.com
- Excite   http://www.excite.com
- The Internet Sleuth   http://www.geocities.com/SiliconValley/ Park/2540/index.html
- Lycos   http://a2z.lycos.com
- InfoSeek   http://www.infoseek.com

Keywords to search for: careers, jobs, employment, resumes, job fairs, career fairs. Also look under your job position, industry, target organization or company, geographic location (city/state).

FIGURE 2-4. **On-Line Resume Resources**

If you cannot afford full-time Internet access, there are free stations in many public libraries.

If you are interested in launching your job search into cyberspace, research which ISP's are vying for customers in your area; look in the science section of your local newspapers, the yellow pages, or in university or alternative local newspapers. Many offer free test drives and software. (Speaking of test drives, it's a good idea to e-mail yourself your resume to check for product quality. If you post your resume on a newsgroup or website, call up your resume, print a copy, and check it out. Also, do a keyword search just as a possible employer would to see if—and how—your resume comes up. Most websites that offer free resume postings will allow you access to edit or update your resume.)

Establish an on-line working strategy:

1. Answer the questions: Why am I on-line? What am I looking for? Do I want to network? Do I want to look for job postings or employers to send my resume to, or try to find places to post my resume? Depending on where you are and the ISP's pricing policies, on-line services and telephone charges can add up. Set limits as to when you want to go on-line, how often, and what your budget is. It is easy to get totally lost on the Web and have a great time, but still have no job.

2. Visit the on-line sites to get a feel for what the various commercial job search sites offer. Take notes as to what is offered, prices, types of jobs or resumes listed (e.g., mostly technical positions or mostly entry-level). Look at resumes in your field if offered for free (many sites charge to view resumes; that's how they support the site).

3. Keep a list of keywords and key phrases and update it regularly. Look for more. If a keyword *"tv and/or video"* brings up resumes or further sites, are there other keywords present? Or is it a poor choice, bringing up information on the *"I Love Lucy* Video Archives"? Perhaps a better strategy would to be search under skills or equipment used: *Beta, Avid.* Keep track of the keywords that work for you.

4. Many sites have Read Me files containing information on topics of interest, such as Interviewing Techniques. Take advantage of these. Don't sit there with the clock ticking though; print the file if it looks good and read it later, off-line.

5. When you are stuck, ask for help. Technical help from your service provider or practical help from other users is available. Try newsgroups for new on-line users or the advice areas in some of the commercial job search sites.

Pat Jones' resume has been redone again (Fig. 2-5) for submission to one of the websites offering free resume posting.

Another alternative, if you are technologically adept, is to create a website of your own. If you use a site to illustrate your talents, you can refer to it in your resume. Instead of mentioning references or stating that your portfolio is available, you could say *Visit my website http://PJones.com/.* Obviously, this ap-

Pat Jones
77 Boxer Street
New York, New York 10012
212-477-1234   Fax 212-477-1235
E-Mail pjones@jones.com

KEYWORDS:
Production Assistant, 3 years' newspaper experience, college graduate, Quark XPress, Adobe PhotoShop, PageMaker, Illustrator, MSPublisher, Windows95/NT, mechanicals, board work, pre-production experience

OBJECTIVE:
Newspaper production assistant utilizing 3 years' on-the-job training; willing to relocate.

SKILLS:
2 years' experience with Quark XPress, Adobe PhotoShop,PageMaker and Illustrator; able to do mechanicals and paste-ups. Pre-production experience.

EXPERIENCE:
CTPress   Oxford, NY   1993-1996
Production assistant at weekly newspaper responsible for designing clients' ads and preparing boards for print. Handled client base of over 50 accounts. Upgraded press' computer software; Windows95/NT. Initiated training of 5 member staff on network.

Intern — Production assistant   1992-1993
Work-study program affiliated with Barton College.
Assisted in design and production of client ads; liaised with print department.

EDUCATION:
Barton College   Oxford, NY   BA, 1995
Teaching Assistant: Communications, Prof. D. Edmunds, 1996-present.

Editor: "Barton Bugle"   1994-1995
Responsible for producing monthly campus newsletter; designed layout and prepared ads on MSPublisher.

Production Manager: 1996 Barton Yearbook

Seminars: Microsoft Print, Jan. 1996

FIGURE 2-5. Sample On-Line Resume

proach will only be effective with employers who are also on-line. (You can do a search for organizations' names to determine if they host websites or advertise on the Internet.)

If you have Internet access, visit David Rodman's site at http://shoga.wwa.com/~roddy/. David's resume (shown in Fig. 2-6)preceded his web site and the site is a work-in-progress. Updated resumes and stationery can refer to his homepage. This is an example of showing a portfolio to potential employers, who can "visit" at their convenience. This site allows for the "selling" of different aspects of Dave's work, as well as for the opportunity to contact him by e-mail.

Alternative Resumes—A Critical Decision

If we can expand our understanding of what a resume can be to "the information you send an employer that describes what you can do for the organization" in the hope of getting a job interview, then the door is open to many other creative approaches. (Notice that the definition is not limited to a paper sent in the mail with a cover letter; you may have a hard copy of your resume but it may go out into cyberspace to be stored in someone else's database.) In many professions, these alternative approaches are the norm.

What You See Is What You Get

If you are a model, actor, performer, or perhaps a musician, your face is an inherent part of your resume. It is not only your written credentials but your look that will get you an interview or audition. Eight by ten glossies, with a written resume on the back, are what the employers expect to see from you. Creativity need not be limited to the choosing of a photograph; the written portion can be intriguing, too.

Samples of your work can make up a greater portion of your resume. A resume can be seen as a presentation piece if you are in the visual arts. Photographers, artists, architects, illustrators, and graphic designers, for example, can get an employer's attention by including or incorporating samples of their work. One great example of showing what you can do in more than words is David Rodman's resume (Fig. 2-6). As you can see from David's resume, the addition of graphics can supplement the written portion of the resume to great effect. Remember that the quality of the printing must be excellent.

FIGURE 2-6. David Rodman's Resume

Attention Getters

A newspaper writer may develop a resume with a headline and newspaper format. Someone looking for a job in public relations may issue a resume in the form of a press release. There may even have been a chef somewhere who has written a resume in icing on a cake! If you are in a creative industry, explore all the alternatives offered to you.

More Is More

Are you going to go for a 2- to 3-page resume? Are you worried that the pages will get lost? (Do not staple.) One terrific resume we saw recently was in the form of a booklet printed on 11 × 17 paper, folded in half. The cover contained the applicant's name and address, and a brief highlight section to get the reader's attention. Inside, on two pages with plenty of white space, was the rest of the resume. It was creative and well-written and it got results—an interview was scheduled.

Other Alternative Ideas

- A three-fold pamphlet.
- A mini-portfolio in a small binder.
- A trading card submitted as a resume to a sports entertainment company.
- Specialized letterhead or business cards. One resume we saw recently included the candidate's photo as part of the letterhead (he was applying for a job as a singer).
- Use of gimmicks such as magnets attached to the letterhead.
- Unusual but appropriate formats. If you are a talent agent, for example, try a resume that looks like *Playbill*. A cartoonist has submitted a resume that is in essence a comic strip. Others in creative fields have done mock-up products for a prospective employer or have created ads for themselves. One candidate for a global sports entertainment company cast himself as a professional wrestler, able to beat all up-and-coming opponents for the job of head of creative services.
- Use of specialized or designer papers, either 8½ × 11 or 3-fold pamphlets; papers with colored borders, accents, or textures.

For some professions and careers, there may be other norms to follow or you may be forced to keep up with what the competition is offering. One great aspect of using the Internet is the ability to comparison shop—you can literally check out the competition and see their resumes or websites. For more suggestions, see Fig. 2-7.

Get Started

Now that you have all the basic information about yourself, know where you are sending your resume(s) to, and know how they will be processed, write a draft of your resume using one

Performers	**Actors, some musicians, TV/radio personalities** *"What you see is what you get"* Personal photo(s)—head shot or composites attached to the back of the resume (or resume printed diectly on the back of the photo), physical description. Defined further by roles cited, places performed in. Influenced by those worked with in past. Offer performance tapes, videos.
Wordsmiths	**Writers, copywriters, marketers, songwriters** *"They live by their words."* Content extremely important; expect you to be word-sensitive. Defined by publishers, clients. Influenced by those worked with in past. Offer writing samples, published excerpts, portfolio.
Artists	**Artists, graphic artists, designers, photographers** *"Putting it on the line."* Form must be A1. Presentation counts. This is what you do—so show off. Enhanced by incorporating samples of work, printing resume on the back of composite, mini-portfolio of best work that matches the would-be client/employer's needs and/or style. Perception influenced by past associations, education. Offer samples, portfolio.
The Media	**Video/TV/film/theater production, direction, or editing** *"Let me show you what I can do."* Content extremely important. Presentation important, judges your professional eye. Listing of credits or credentials essential. Perception influenced by past associations, education. Offer samples, portfolio, referrals to public works, publications, websites.

FIGURE 2-7. Alternative Resumes

of the three basic formats. You have made a lot of decisions about targeting your resume and marketing yourself. Now it's time to actually write it.

Writing Hints

Use terms that are common to the job but avoid unnecessary jargon. You want to let the reader know that you are an insider, but you don't want to go over the edge with acronyms, abbreviations, and technical terms. Make sure any terms you use are state of the art or at the very least current. For example, New Media is the term of choice as we go to print, but how long that term will continue in use remains to be seen as this whole new industry continues to redefine itself. Remember that your resume may be read by a gatekeeper (a human or a computer) using a check-off list to screen resumes.

Include related, transferable skills. Show all the skills you can bring with you. Remember, less is more. You need to decide what to include and what to leave out. Even though you may be impressed that you have won the Ancient Mariner Award, and everyone who knows about it knows it was tough to accomplish, if the reader may be ignorant of this prestigious but esoteric award, you should omit it. At the same time, accomplishments that seemed effortless to you but pack an organizational wallop should be included without hesitation. Ask colleagues to help you bring these victories to the surface once more.

Use action-oriented verbiage. Show that you *can* do (because you already have) and your enthusiasm and experience will show that you *will* do (even more ... bigger ... better) for the new employer lucky enough to attract you.

Keep it as simple as possible. Make every word count. Rather than say *"I have developed...,"* just say *"... developed...."* Drop off the helping verbs and the word *"I"*; the reader knows the resume is about your accomplishments and it's all about you.

Keep your tenses straight. When writing about your present job, do not write in the past tense; this can sound as if you've already quit working there and all your accomplishments are in the past.

Highlight those skills and experiences essential to the job opening. Do it in your resume and in your cover letter. Make a comparison chart:

ABC Inc. needs	**I can provide**
▪ a features writer.	▪ timely coverage of issues of interest to the boomer generation that comprises 80% of your readership
▪ a writer with excellent grammar.	▪ skills honed in the English Department earning a BA at Baruch College, further developed in 8 years writing for Bluebook Magazine.
▪ a writer who can meet deadlines.	▪ excellent organizational skills and technical expertise, using MAC-based programs.
▪ a writer who can develop own leads and stories.	▪ valuable contacts in diverse fields that have led me to publish stories on health, childcare, sports, entertainment and politics.

Use words like "my team," "we," and "my department" to show you are a team player.

Act as if you are a part of the new organization already. Show fit by referring to jobs, organizations, and experiences in your resume that are similar to the prospective employer.

Pay attention to word choice. For hand-processed resumes, concentrate on verbs; for scanned or electronic resumes, use nouns for keywords.

Pay attention to grammar. Do not switch tenses. Simple sentences are preferred to complex; think sound bites.

Use your own voice. Do not write "meticulous" instead of "orderly" unless that is how you really talk.

Don't ask for a "challenging position." This puts the onus on the employer to keep you happy, challenged, and motivated. Leave the reader with the perception that you create your own challenges and are motivated to continue to do so.

Sample Resumes

As a guide and inspiration, sample resumes are included after Chapter 3. Also, a Creative Menu for Resumes summarizing all the permutations of choice appears in Fig. 2-8.

Possibilities	Your Decisions	Manually processed	Internet posted	Scanned	Faxed
Chronological Functional Combined	Choices of format:	Open	Open	Open	Open
Centered Flush left, right Bulleted Lines, half-lines	Choices of layout:	Open	• No bold • No underlining • No italics • Flush left • 64-70 character spaces wide	• No bold • No underlining • No italics	• No underlining
White & shades of white, cream pastels, brights marbled textures watermarks	Choices of paper:	Open	None (if mailed, strong, white stock-unfolded)	Strong, white stock-unfolded	Strong, white stock-unfolded
Include or not "Clip Art" or original	Choices of graphics:	Open	None, unless HTML/JAVA scripted; own web page	None	Limited to simple black/white
Serif, sans-serif Bold, italics, small caps "Fancy" fonts Symbols	Choices of type/font:	Open	Plain text or ASCII	• Clear, legible • Sans serif • 10 pt or larger	• Clear, legible • Avoid "thin" fonts e.g., Impact • 10 pt or larger
Photos-self Photos-work Work samples	Choices of attachments	Open	None	None	Limited
Booklets, folders, special designs	Choices for alternative formats	Open	None or Web page	None	Limited

Scanned or faxed resumes: Much is dependent on quality of software and equipment. Sending photos, artwork, or graphics could backfire if employer's printer distorts image. Send a test fax to a friend and/or do a test scan to determine quality of output.

Internet posted resumes: Test post your resume. Call it up and retrieve a copy. Check quality and accuracy of output.

FIGURE 2-8. Creative Menu for Resumes

The sample resumes included in the last section of this book are *possible* resumes for various professions, and are not presented to indicate the precise qualifications needed for these jobs. It is the creative approach to the presentation of information in these resumes that you should focus on.

Summary

Proofread ... Proofread ... Proofread!

Read your resume aloud. Spell check programs on computers will not pick up "principal/principle" mistakes. This has been said before but it cannot be stressed enough: Having misspelled words on your resume is like going to an interview with something stuck between your front teeth ... that may be all the interviewer sees!!!

Pay Attention to All the Details

Margins should be approximately 1″ on all sides. If your resume does not fill up a complete page, increase the side and bottom margins to 1¼″ or 1½″.

Line spacing should be consistent: single, double, or 1.5 × between lines or sections. Establish a pattern and keep to it.

Punctuation should also be the same throughout the resume. One space or two after periods? Choose one style and use it consistently.

Sections and paragraphs must be aligned properly. Tabs, indents, left or right justification, centered alignment? Be consistent—establish a pattern that is held up in the entire document. Have elements lined up, such as dates, locations, job titles. After you have printed up a draft copy, check your alignment with a ruler if necessary. If the person reading your resume has an eye for detail (and feels that is an essential requisite for the job), you can upset your chances by having skewed indents or unaligned columns. You do have the chance to be perfect with your resume so show off all your abilities.

Paper choice should support and enhance your resume. Don't go for bright yellow if you are a blue serge type. If you go for texture or laid paper, look for the watermark—it should face you when you read the copy. Consider all the ranges of cream, white, off-white, gray, and blue. If you are including photos, artwork or other work samples, consider a glossy paper.

Do not let your resume leave a first impression of you as someone who cannot spell correctly, or who offers a confused, jumbled presentation, or who does not care about the details.

Color can be used if used wisely. Including color photos or color copies can sell you if the quality is good. So can adding color touches, consistently, in bullets, lines, background, or shaded graphics. Do not overwhelm—if an employer wants to see your portfolio, you will be invited for an interview!

- When appropriate, **use bold text, italics, underlining, indents, bullets, white space, or symbols** to break up the text. (Use bullets approximately the same size as lower case letters.) Make your resume easy to follow and easy on the eye. If you want to see if it looks balanced graphically, look at it upside-down or in a mirror to concentrate on the shape of the text rather than the words themselves.

- **Use lines, half-lines, borders, different fonts, or graphics** to enhance your text. See the sample resumes for choices.

- **Control yourself creatively.** Do not get so caught up with your creative urges (or all the fonts your software has to offer) that your resume looks like a typographer's sample sheet. Two or three type faces in a document are usually enough to provide visual interest and impact. The same goes for type size. You need not go to a

30 point text

to emphasize a point. Nor should you feel that using a

6 point font

will allow you to sneak in more information on one page.

- If you have the content to include in your sales pitch, **extend your resume to more than one page.** Do not just include 2 or 3 lines on the second page; spread it out visually and logically. Try not to split up areas of information. Do not staple pages together; the reader will want to look at them side by side to get the entire story. Likewise, do not carry text over to the reverse side of the page: It may be missed entirely. Note "continued" on the bottom of the first page and your name along with "page 2 of 2" on the top of the second page.

- **Be professional.** Your resume and cover letter should be creative and visually appealing, but it is the content that will get you the interview.

- **Target your cover letter and resume** to the job opening and the organization. Your approach should be customer-driven. Writing the resume and cover letter and researching the organization and job opening are all preparatory to an interview—the reason for all these preliminary activities. Do not forget that, as much as you think you may want the job offer, your research into the organization and the information you gain in an interview is to help *you* consider whether or not you would actually like to work there.

- **Follow up.** If you state in your cover letter that you will telephone in four days or next week, do so. Even if you are not invited for an interview, inquire in a friendly (not confrontational) manner about how your resume fit with the job opening, and whether it will be kept on file in case further job openings occur.

3

Presenting a Complete Package

A resume is a document that requires great time and attention to develop, and then must be used only in an appropriate manner. Customization to the job applied for and a customer focus are two basic and essential considerations. But another important aspect to address is the manner of its introduction, which requires that you consider two questions carefully: what is to be included and who will the recipient be? As we have said previously, even the most presentable resume should not travel alone. Ideally, you should always find an excuse to delay its presentation until you have the opportunity to present it in person. Barring personal delivery, the mail (or any other approach that you use when you are unable to deliver the resume in person) will have to suffice. In these situations, each resume should be accompanied by a cover letter.

As with the resume, there is no room for error in a cover letter. In addition to the research that you performed so you could customize the resume for the organization to which it is being presented, you need to learn the name and title of the person to whom the cover letter (and resume) should be addressed. It should go without saying that the correct spelling of the name, title, organization name, and address are imperative; we mention it here to ensure that this requirement is given its due. Consider the cover letter as the first part of your sales package—explaining to the reader concisely what position you wish to be considered for and why you are the ideal candidate.

A more accurate term for this correspondence would be a *marketing letter*. It serves a very important purpose because it is intended to be read first. If the cover letter is boring, what chance for attention can the resume (or you) have?

Whom Should You Send a Marketing Letter To?

Remember the research you did to determine which organizations you would like to target in an effort to land a job? You need to take one more step before sending them your material. A little more research here will go a long way. In fact, this entry point is a make or break situation. How many "Dear Sir or Madam" letters do you think the HR department gets daily? If you targeted XYZ Inc., call their offices in advance to determine the exact name and title of the person you should send your resume to. Do not ask for a job, or what positions are open, or even whether there are any openings. Just get the correct name and title of the person to contact and be sure the spelling of both are accurate. You never want to have the chance to blame the person you spoke to on the phone for providing inaccurate information. You also need to find out if the company accepts resumes by fax or e-mail. (And if they do, then you need the correct fax number or again, all will be lost.)

"Resumes Are the Junk Mail of the Nineties"

That is what one frustrated human resources professional stated recently because of the proliferation of resumes received since fax machines have grown in popularity. Now, add electronic mail to that phenomenon!

You need to keep your resume from being lumped into the "junk" category. To avoid a futile trip into the circular file, your job search efforts must now focus on the organizations that you are targeting as recipients of your terrific resume. Now, in preparation for selling that resume to the desired organizations, you need to turn your attention to the companies again.

Target a few organizations and learn as much about them and their key players as you can. Go back to our earlier discussion on networking and consider who you know in any of the organizations that you have initially decided to target. Look for news stories and articles that mention your targeted organizations. In addition to confirming your belief in the viability of the organization and its prospects for growth, any articles you find regarding the organization you wish to join will provide you with additional material to strengthen your resume and cover letter.

Dear Who?

The rule to follow here is go with your biggest fan first or, in the absence of anyone you know, go to the most senior person with knowledge of or responsibility for your specific area of expertise. If you are a graphic designer, sending a letter and resume to the vice president of the Creative Services Department will give you visibility with the person who knows what that department's problems are and what technical expertise is needed to solve them. A similar package sent to the chairman of the board or the senior HR professional may or may not get you a hearing, because neither may understand your resume or be able to link it to Creative Services. Do not forget about the back doors into organizations. If you know an attorney for the organization (on staff or even outside counsel), a client or vendor, or even a relative or neighbor who works there, talk to that person to determine whether he or she is receptive to your candidacy and to evaluate whether that person could effectively introduce you to the organization.

Data regarding any organization you wish to join is getting easier to obtain daily. The burden is on you to find the information. Indices in the print media provide lists of all the organizations mentioned in the business pages of newspapers and trade journals. Websites allow you to find information regarding almost any organization you might wish to join.

Talk up your interest, too, as often as possible because you need to enlist the support of anyone who may become an information resource for you. More than ever, we need assistance in finding the needles of information we want in the haystacks of data available to us.

The Marketing Letter Is the Preamble to Your Resume

The marketing letter directs the reader to the specific information contained in your resume. This is the letter that you send to all your leads, contacts, and job referrals; to answer blind or classified ads; or to ask friends to refer you to others who may have job openings. The marketing letter must be as customer-driven as your resume. Remember that the only purpose for contacting these individuals is to get an interview to get the job!

Should You Mail a Resume?

Most jobs come from referrals, from networking with everyone who could possibly help you find a job. Only a small percentage of jobs (approximately 20 percent according to recruiters) are filled through classified ads. Mass mailings account for even less. But you only need one job! You should not rule out mailing marketing letters and your resume to unknowns, but these wild shots (consider them also as cold calls) should not be a major portion of your job search. Your time will be better spent if you take the initiative to research leads and jobs, then send targeted, directed marketing letters as a follow-up to those specific opportunities. Too often, cover letters and resumes are written from the point of view of the applicant (the writer) rather than the employer (the recipient). These letters should be considered teasers, giving enough information so readers want to know more about you, but not so much that they don't need (or want!) any more. You have to cast yourself as the solution to a reader's problems.

It is best to delay handing over your resume until the last minute, preferably in person, at the interview. That is the ideal situation—to have gotten the interview on the strength of a referral, a lead that you have followed, or a dynamic marketing letter. Even though that is the ideal, practically there are many situations in which you are asked to mail a resume directly (in order to qualify for an interview). Some of the leads you are following will warrant a mailing of your resume. Send the resume, but do not let it travel alone. Include an equally dynamic, targeted cover letter.

What Is in a Marketing Letter?

The gist of the marketing letter is that if the reader lets you slip through his or her fingers, certain calamity will befall the organization as you are the *ideal* candidate and can do for the organization what no one else can do (just short of leaping tall buildings).

Essentially, there are three main areas or points to be covered in a marketing letter:

1. An introductory, attention-getting opener that should let reader know why you are writing. *When I read in the* Wall Street Journal *that you were expanding your advertising campaign into radio ads, I knew that my experience would be ideal*

to support your efforts in this area to increase your market share. Or *Sam Jones, your sales manager, recommended that I contact you regarding the opening in your graphics department. Sam and I have worked together in the past and he felt that my experience and talents would be ideal for ABC Company.* Now, add some details regarding your skills and experience to entice the reader.

2. Explain why you are the solution to the reader's immediate and long-range problems. State your qualifications crisply and succinctly. *If you want a cutting-edge presence on-line with fully-interactive websites and state-of-the-art 3D graphics, we must discuss our future together.* Or *The essence of breaking into foreign markets is an understanding of the culture, the potential customer's mindset, and the traditional (and nontraditional) methods of capturing their disposable income. These are my specific areas of expertise. I have increased market share for my current employer over 30% in the past 18 months.* Support your claims with specific, quantified examples. Give them the "Can do—Will do" approach.

3. The closing—what action will be taken. *On Thursday morning, November 5th, I will telephone you to set up a convenient time to discuss this matter further. If you cannot wait until then, call me at your convenience.* Just be sure to call if you promise to.

Marketing Letter Details

Every marketing letter should include the following:

- **Complete and accurate name of the organization and individual**, spelled correctly, and with the appropriate title. Call the organization to determine accuracy, including gender. Make sure that when you get the information, it is correct as to both spelling and title accuracy. Call back and speak to the person's assistant, especially if that was not the person you spoke to the first time. You may have been speaking to a temp covering the reception phone who didn't have complete information. Avoid the hackneyed "Dear Sir or Madam." If you cannot spend the time to determine who should get your resume and cover letter and the correct way to address that person, what does that say about your candidacy?

- **Accurate designation or title of the position for which you wish to apply.** Think "you" instead of "I" to make the letter customer-driven. Write in your own voice. Do not say "Contained herewith is my resume for your esteemed consideration" unless that is how you normally talk. Do not write a bouncy, peppy letter if you are a dyed-in-the-wool buttoned-down type. Say exactly enough ("Please consider me for the position of graphic designer") and add a few choice phrases as to why you can be the perfect addition to the company's staff. Do not rephrase your entire life story.

- **Be complete.** Do not abbreviate St. for Street, NYC for New York City.

- **Propose a plan of action.** Do not say *If you are seeking a person with my qualifications ...* but rather *I will telephone you in a week....* Plan a follow-up and then carry it out! Do not leave the ball entirely in their court.

- **Be original.** Everyone says *Sincerely yours* or *Yours truly* to close a letter. Seek alternatives: *Wishing you the best, With confidence.* Be creative.

- **Use a blank envelope when sending letters to cold calls.** Avoid using labels—they scream "mass mailing" and your letter must get past the gatekeeper. Figure out how to get the printer to print right on the envelope. If you can't, get assistance or use a typewriter.

Two sample marketing letters are included for you to review, one for a specific ad (Fig. 3-1) and another for a more general approach (Fig. 3-2) from the Webmaster applicant.

Getting Even More Creative

Just as you have not ignored the look of your resume, do not pass up the chance to present a sharp marketing letter. It must be clean—no typos, corrections, mistaken creases, or smudges. Obviously, it should not have crossed-out changes in your telephone number(s) or address or anything else including date, title, and name changes!

Consider the following to make a positive impression:

- Coordinated letterhead or stationery for cover letter and resume. Sources such as PAPER DIRECT (1-800-A-PAPERS) or PAPER ACCESS (1-800-PAPER01) provide catalogs with choices for business cards, stationery, fax forms, and designer papers to use with your home computer and printer.

PAT JONES
77 BOXER STREET
NEW YORK, NEW YORK 10012
212-477-1234   FAX 212-477-3732

November 4, 1996

Mr. Allan Smith
Director of Personnel
ABC Organization
987 Main Street
New York, New York 10001

Dear Mr. Smith,

Sunday's edition of **The New York Times** (10/27/96) carried your advertisement for an <u>**Art Director**</u>. My resume is attached and I would like you to consider me for the position for the following reasons:

◆ Over 15 years of experience as an artist, designer and art director at major advertising agencies in New York and Connecticut;
◆ Handles projects from concept, through all phases of design and comprehensives, to finished mechanicals or final film;.
◆ Excellent rapport with clients and design team members proven by 15% increase in billings over past 9 months; and
◆ Management experience with staff of 15 designers.

As further proof of my qualifications for the position, consider the following ad campaigns I have developed over the past 2 years; I feel they are as good as, if not better than, programs you have released over a similar period of time.

"Nike Sportswear...Don't Just Do It...Look Good Doing It"
"PC World...at your fingertips"
"Vintage Seltzer"   Streams flowing into bottles (animated)
Chase Manhattan Bank (acquisition by Chemical Bank)

To look at my "book" and to discuss how we can work together in the future, we must get together. I will call your office on November 15th to arrange a convenient time. Should you wish to speak to me earlier, I can be reached at the above numbers at any time.

Until we speak,

Pat Jones

FIGURE 3-1. Cover Letter Sample 1

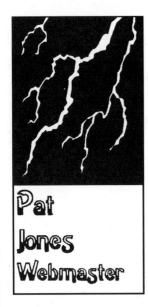

77 Boxer Street
Bedford Hills, NY
10516-1703
(914)477-1234
E-mail pjones@jones.com
http://www.patj/jones.com
http://www.tryus.com

May 7, 1997

Ms. Nanette F. Guenther
Vice President, Technology
2001 Corporation, Inc.
1 Prince Street
New York, New York 10023

Dear Ms. Guenther:

This is your lucky day. It is not every day that great applicants for
employment at XYZ Corporation come to your attention.

The other day I learned that you have been seeking a Webmaster
with little success. Enclosed is my resume. The variety of experiences
I have had in environments similar to yours—namely state of the art
in technology, entrepreneurial and involved in every level—make me
a serious candidate.

I will call you on Monday to arrange a meeting at a mutually
convenient time.

Let me take this opportunity to thank you for your interest and attention
and to assure you that the time you spend meeting with me will be
well spent.

Looking forward to talking with you,

Pat Jones

FIGURE 3-2. Cover Letter Sample 2

- Envelopes pre-printed with your return address.

- Typed or laser-printed addresses on envelopes (not handwritten unless you are a letterer or calligrapher). No labels: They scream *Mass mailing!*

- Use a presentation folder. Include your cover letter, resume, and samples of your work in a neat folder.

- Allow some color to enter into your presentation, either through work samples, stationery, or spot color in your letter or resume. With prices falling for color printers, this option is becoming more possible. Of course, the quality of the color printing should be excellent, or leave it out.

When Is a Cover Letter Not a Cover Letter?

If you send your resume by fax, do not let a shoddy, poor quality cover sheet precede it. Whether you are using a modem or a separate fax machine, establish an attractive, coordinated, eye-catching fax layout. If you use a modem it is easy to have several fax templates ready.

Follow the same rules for faxed cover sheets as for scanned resumes—not too fancy with the typefaces or symbols. Try a test run if you have any doubts. Include the same points as you would in a cover letter. See Fig. 3-3 for a sample fax cover sheet for Pat Jones, Public Affairs Director. This fax was meant to be the cover letter for the resume for Public Affairs Director found in the sample resume section. Since Pat is an on-air personality and has approached the employer by means of an introduction from a member of his team, Pat has adopted a very cordial approach and has sent a fax photo along with the resume. There is ample justification for including a small sample of your work, a definitive logo, or other graphic in the fax cover sheet to tie it to you and your resume. But be certain to do a "test run" first to check for clarity.

Follow Up on All Your Resumes

When you send resumes, always follow up with a telephone call. Feel free to ask what the employer thought of your resume. Did it meet the job's qualifications? Was it clear and easy to follow? Ask for comments on improving it.

When you present your resume in person, ask for feedback. If you were asked for an interview there must have been

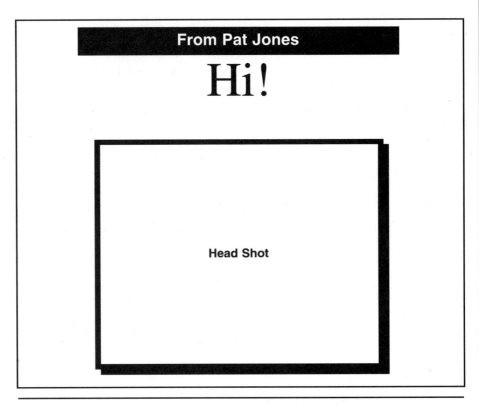

From Pat Jones

Hi!

Head Shot

Date: 10/30/96	Pages to follow: 2

To: D. J. Cannon Director of Programming	201-555-1212

RTGB-TV
Princeton, NJ

From: Pat Jones	212-477-1235

Comments:

Bob Evans, your news manager, has recommended that I send you my resume so you can consider me for the position of Public Affairs Director. With over 20 years of experience in TV—from production to on-air host to my current position as Public Affairs Director—I certainly have the "ratings" to fill the position. Bob thought that I would fit right in with your team and from watching your recent changes in programming, I feel that there is an element of synergy we should definitely explore.

I will call you on Wednesday to discuss the position further. I am live on Channel 34 at 1:00 PM daily, just on the off chance you are one of the few who may have not seen the show!

Looking forward to talking to you.

Pat Jones

If you do not receive all of these pages, please call 212-475-1234.

FIGURE 3-3. Fax Sample

something that intrigued the employer. Did you lead them astray (were they expecting Steven Spielberg)? No resume is written in stone; always seek to fine-tune it. Do not spend more time on your resume or cover letter than you do on any other aspect of your job search, but give them both as much attention as they need. Consider each of them a work in progress.

Summary

You have spent a lot of time and energy designing and writing your resume. Invest as much in your cover letter.

- Your cover letter *must* be customer-driven.
- It should be addressed to the specific source of the job opening: Make reference to the advertisement, job posting on the Internet, or lead that you are following up on.
- State the job opening or area of employment you are asking to be considered for; don't make the reader wait too long for the punch line (*What does this one want?*).
- The same rules that generally apply to resumes—concise, to-the-point writing style intended to intrigue the reader—apply to cover letters. The word "intrigue" has been used specifically because the intention of a resume and cover letter is to pique the reader's interest. The prospective employer should have enough information about you to want to know more—to request an interview!
- Ask for an interview. Tell the reader that you will follow up to arrange it.
- Review each letter to consider what worked and what didn't. There is no need to start each new letter from scratch. Use what has been effective and get rid of those items that haven't worked.

Resumes

1. Actor
2. Actor/Sound Effects Specialist
3. Advertising Producer
4. Animator
5. Animator: Computer
6. Antiques Consultant
7. Antiques Dealer
8. Architect
9. Art Department Coordinator
10. Art Director
11. Artist
12. Artist/Interior Designer
13. Arts Administrator
14. Associate Television Producer
15. Audio Designer
16. Author (Scanned)
17. Broadcast Journalist
18. Broadcast Producer
19. Calligrapher (Freelance)
20. Caterer
21. Chef: Pastry (Entry-level)
22. Color Consultant (Freelance)
23. Commercial Artist
24. Costume Designer
25. Creative Director/Graphic Design
26. Dancer/Singer
27. Digital Artist/3D Animator (Scanned)
28. Entertainment Producer
29. Events Planner (Freelance)
30. Fashion Coordinator

31. Figure Skating Instructor
32. Film/Video Producer (Freelance)
33. Golf Pro
34. Graphic Designer (Entry-level)
35. Graphic Designer (Freelance)
36. Graphic Designer (Part-time, On-line posted)
37. Hair Stylist
38. Hotel Concierge
39. Interior Designer
40. Jewelry Designer (Freelance)
41. Lighting and Audio Designer
42. Location Scout
43. Multimedia Developer (On-line version)
44. Multimedia Producer
45. Multimedia Producer/CD-ROM
46. Music Composer—Computer
47. Musician (Freelance)
48. New Media Content Manager
49. News Broadcast Reporter
50. Photographer
51. Photographer's Stylist
52. Photographer—Journalist
53. Private Investigator
54. Production Designer
55. Public Affairs Director (Faxed)
56. Public Relations/Marketing Manager
57. Publicist
58. Recreation Director
59. Restaurant Manager
60. Screenwriter/Television Producer (Freelance)
61. Set Decorator
62. Set Designer
63. Sports Commentator
64. Stunt Coordinator (Freelance)
65. Television Director (Freelance)
66. Television Off/On-line Editor
67. Television Producer
68. Television Production Coordinator
69. Theatrical Director (Entry-level)
70. Trade Show & Set Designer
71. Travel Agent
72. Travel Consultant/Tour Operator
73. TV Production Facility Manager
74. Webmaster
75. Writer/Producer/Director (Freelance)

Pat Jones

SAG   AFTRA   AEA
77 Boxer Street
New York, New York 10012
212-477-1234   Fax 212-477-1235

Height: 5'4"   Weight: 115   Eyes: Brown   Hair: Ash Blonde

☆ **Film:**

One Wish	Upscale shopper	Ute Horvinges
Wichie Woman	Mother of Tom Hanks	Bob Howard
Yikes ... the Ducks!	Gwen Robbins	Bob Howard
Una Notte'	Cybeleline	Jenna Da Vinci
Geriantics	Mrs. Fritsel	Bob Howard

☆ **Theater:**

Due North	Anna May	Sergio Leone
Heaven Only	Mother	Berden Deiogrt
Broadway Repertory		Susan and Bill Evans
Vanities	Rebecca	Elvira Tannin

☆ **Television:**

Urban Decay	Narrator	Gregory Norris
Soapsuds	Nurse	Various
One Way to Love	Emily	Various
Specific Dangers	Homeless woman	Bob Howard

☆ **Training:**

Acting:	Gwen deVry, Willy Holden, Mary Monti
Voice:	Deborah French, "Ace" Williams

☆ **Special Skills:**   Fluent in German, French, Spanish
Gymnast, In-line Skating, Figure Skating
Mime, Dialects, Impersonations

☆ **Awards:**   "Broadway Best," 1995

Video and/or Audio tape available.

You know me.
You may not
know my
face.

But...
You know ME!

Pat Jones
77 Boxer Street
New York, New York
10012

212-477-1234
212-477-1235 Fax

PROFESSIONAL HISTORY
1991–present
Freelance
Performed in various commercials, audio tapes, voice-overs for clients located in US and South America.

Specialize in sound effects, dialects, strange accents and characters.

Will be the voice of "Pucky" for the NY Islanders Hockey Team for the 1997–1998 season.

Develop original characters and voices to suit client needs.

1989–1991
Universal Studios Animation Labs
Character Consultant

Created voices for over 100 different animated "characters" in 35 short films.

Recorded sounds and stories for Universal Studios, Florida
"Back to the Future—the Ride"
"Jaws—the Ride"

1987–1989
Actor
Appeared in several commercials, off-off-Broadway plays, and professional theater groups on East Coast.

EDUCATION
University of Chicago, 1986
Liberal Arts

I am
the sound of the squeaky wheel in the Reebok commercial, "Rolling Over Your Competition"; and

the happy shopping cart in Disney's "The Elves in the Shopping Mall."

I am
the announcer for the Cosmos Soccer team; and

the voice of "Milk" in the Drakes Cakes commercial; and

the background noise (all of it) in WPLJ "Scam '96" CD.

I am
the voices on "101 Crazy Messages to Put on Your Answering Machine" audio tape; and

the sound of the unearthly creatures in Smashing Pumpkins' video "Over My Head."

I am
the sound effects (yes ... even the storm and the fire) in Stephen King's "New York: Terror Town" audio tape.

I am
1,000,000 different sounds and voices, musical instruments, animals, forces of nature, electrical devices and more.

ADVERTISING PRODUCER

Pat Jones

77 Boxer Street
New York, New York
10012
212-477-3732

What I Want

Position as advertising manager in agency willing to be first in the market, gain more new clients and keep old ones increasing their billings.

Where I Have Been

De Luca, Guenther and Brown, New York City

1988–Present	Producer of Special Projects
1982–1986	Assoc. Producer/Video Editor
1980–1982	Asst. Communications Manager

Who I Am

Knowledgeable advertising producer, highly motivated, and up to any challenge.

Unflappable and reliable in the face of deadlines, keeping new business operations and the administration of my department on schedule and within budget.

A seasoned professional with start to finish production expertise, sensitive to the processes and personalities of advertising, and especially to the creative department.

What I Do

Produce broadcast, test and radio commercials which include livematics, animatics as claymation, as well as TV billboard ID's for all DG&B clients.

Assist in developing ideas leading to production of hot ticket items such as saving and most importantly winning accounts.

New business creative work: clients include TIMEX, BLOOMINGDALE'S, SOUTH STREET SEAPORT, KIWI AIR, DKNY, APPLE BANK, YAHOO!, ARTISTIC PRESS & PAPERS.

Travel to our domestic and international offices to coordinate television spec spots while we pitch new accounts.

Work closely with executive creative director. Implement creative ideas in the form of television commercials and presentation pieces on video tape, hypertext and CD-ROM.

Where I Studied

1987	Advertising/Marketing, Parsons School of Design
1985	Certificate in Film and Tape, Tisch School of the Arts
1982	B.A. Communications, Marymount Manhattan

Call for my reel ... You'll be glad you did.

Pat Jones

Objective

Creative animation position in both print and electronic media environments; experienced in pen & ink, color & background.

Employment Experience

1995–present   **Column Developments, Inc.**   **San Jose, California**
Editor-in-chief for all products developed.
Responsible for staff of 23 animators and writers; annual budget of $1.7M.
* Published *"World of Comix,"* winner of Golden Pencil, 1995
* Consulting editor for all on-line, CD-ROM, and print animated projects
* Animator for *"Guess Who?"*

1992–1993   **MediaQuest Corp.**   **Ridgewood, New Jersey**
Assistant Editor
* Developed 6 new, profitable titles in *"Defenders"* comic line
* Edited and animated *"Thunder Rats"* video game
* Developed on-line and CD-ROM versions of 12 titles in *"AGENT U.S.A."* line.
* Produced popular 1980's *"Babsie"* for comic books and animation

Freelance Experience

1993–present   Animation, scripting, editing, and product development
* *Bub*   New Line Animatics
* *Dark World*   World Vision
* *Adventures of Joe & Joe*   BCO, Inc.
* *NFL, The Game*   NFL
* *StarRoad*   MediaQuest Corp.
* *Budgie & Bowler*   New Line Animatics
* *Cree*   MediaQuest Corp.

Education

University of Southern California   BFA, 1992

Visit my interactive website at http:/pjones.animate.com/2349/USC.

77 Boxer Street   San Jose, California 95112   213-477-1234   Fax 213-477-1235
E-mail pjones@jones.com

Pat Jones

Career Objective: Computer animator specialist using 3-D Studio, Amipro, IPAS, PhotoShop and other related packages.

Professional Highlights:

➤ Production of high quality video graphics and animation sequences.
➤ Experienced in music composition and audio processing.
➤ In-depth knowledge of cutting edge animation software and related graphics packages such as *Vistapro, Fractal Painter, Freehand Graphic Studio, Animator Pro.*
➤ Able to work independently or in a team setting.

Achievements:

➤ Produced over 35 animation sequences ranging from 4.5 sec. to 4 min. for first-run movies such as *"Virtual Kill"* (Paramount), *"The Hackers"* (NewLine), *"James Bond Jr."* (MGM), and *"The 10 Commandments"* (Disney).
➤ Created website animation for 13 top-rated television shows during the 1995–96 season.
➤ 3-D modeler for 4 interactive CD-ROM games
➤ Lead animator on CD-ROM game *"Kennedy"*
➤ Designed titles for *"Meteors," "Craters All Around," "Food in Space,"* and *"We Are Going to Where?"* for NASA/Education

Work History:

| 1993–present | **CompuLabs Animation, Inc.**
Computer Animator/Audio Specialist | Orange, CA |
| 1991–1993 | **Jet Propulsion Lab**
Research Assistant/Education Division | Pasadena, CA |

Education:

| | **Chapel University**
Computer Sciences
➤ 2nd Place Winner: "Student Animated Film Shorts," 1990 | BS, 1990 |
| | Eastman School of Music
Music Composition/Piano | BA, 1986 |

Video tape portfolio available on request.

➤➤➤➤➤➤➤➤➤➤➤➤➤➤

77 Boxer Street   New York, New York 10012
212-477-1234   Fax 212-477-1235   E-mail pjones@jones.com

Pat Jones

Antiques Consultant

Summary:

Twenty years of experience researching, buying, appraising, restoring, repairing and selling original antiques.

Specialization in Oriental & Eastern Asian artworks.

Proven management and sales skills; published writer.

Professional History:

Pat Jones Inc.　　　　**1991–Present**

New York, New York
Founder/President

Manage artwork search and buying service for select corporate and residential clients. Administer appraisal, restoration, repair and sale of original pieces. Maintain relations with top domestic and international galleries.

Gallery Jerusalem　　　　**1986–1991**

New York, New York
Assistant Manager

Planned and executed coordinated sales and marketing effort for newly-formed gallery specializing in Oriental and Eastern Asian artworks. Accompanied owner on buying trips to Orient and Asia to purchase for gallery. Arranged exhibition and sale events at Javits Center for Vietnamese artists living in US.

Sales volume first year $750,000 increasing 128% over 5 year period.

Supervised and trained staff of 3, including bookkeeper.

Independent consultant　　　　**1985–1986**

Asia Society
New York, New York

Responsible for arranging quarterly group shows and exhibits of contemporary and historic Asian art. Wrote monthly column on jewelry for "Asian Art News."

Major project was to repair and restore textile collection. Recommended display and conservation methods.

Education:

New York University　BA, 1984

Minored in Asian Studies

Metropolitan Museum of Art　　　　1984–1986

Special Skills:

Fluent in French and Japanese
Traveled extensively throughout Far East and Asia
Photographer
MS Word, Excel, Quicken

Affiliations:

Asia Society
　　　Slide presentation: "Vietnam's Lost Art," January, 1995
Japan Society
American Society of Antique Dealers
Societe de Antique de Japonique
　　　Guest lecturer: "Enamelware" June, 1996

Interests:

Collection of 17th Century wooden puzzles displayed at World Financial Center, Winter 1994.

insert
color
photo
representing
recent
pieces

77 Boxer Street
New York, New York 10012
212-477-1234 Fax 212-477-1235
Cell 212-678-1234

Pat Jones

77 Boxer Street   New York, New York 10012
212-477-1234

❧ OBJECTIVE ☙

Position as a purchasing agent of early 19th Century antiques, jewelry, china and furniture for a major organization. Expert on English glassware.

❧ EMPLOYMENT ☙

Freelance buyer   **New York City**   **1994 to Present**
Accompany clients to Pennsylvania, Upstate New York and New England to purchase antiques. Travel to England on behalf of private clients to purchase antiques.

Published marketing newsletter *"Everything Old Is New Again"* with a mailing to 1500 subscribers quarterly highlighting upcoming regional auctions.

Yesteryear, Inc.   **Lancaster, PA**   **1990–1994**
Associate buyer for retail/wholesale antique dealer; annual sales volume $2.8M Purchased 19th Century furniture, antique jewelry, glassware and lamps. Attended major auctions to purchase for store, clients and owner's private collection. Authorized to make purchases up to $15,000.

Supported merchandising and customer service in three shops. Supervised sales staff of 12.

Ah-Haa!   **Philadelphia, PA**   **1986–1990**
Co-owner and operator, marketed hand-decorated shirts, bags and hats to the student and tourist population. Shared responsibility for designing, printing, advertising and selling all items.

Summertime, operated a sales cart at Amish Square, Lancaster, PA.
Generated profits that supported 50% of college tuition.

❧ EDUCATION ☙

Pennsylvania State University   **Philadelphia, PA**
Bachelor of Fine Arts   Major: Art History   Minor: History (19th Century)

Guest lecturer at Symposium on English glassware at Antiques '95, Albany.
Attend regional and English seminars and conferences on antiques.

❧ AFFILIATIONS ☙

National Society for the Preservation of Traditional English Glassware
The Wedgwood Society
American Society of Antique Dealers
The Lancaster Society for the Preservation of Amish Arts

ARCHITECT

Pat Jones
77 Boxer Street   New York, New York 10012
212-477-1234   Fax 212-477-1235
E-mail pjones@jones.com

Architect/activist with proven ability and track record completing urban renewal projects in the inner city for the past 12 years. Seeking a position with firm committed to preserving historical past.

ACHIEVEMENTS

● Work featured in Feb. 1995 Architectural Age magazine *"Making the Old New Again."*
● Designed *"Bronx 2000"* project to reclaim section of New York City. Plan cited by Habitat for Humanity for excellent use of resources and preservation of existing structures; $45M government funded.
● Consultant to Greenwich Village Preservation Committee for architectural projects.
● Designed waterfront project for Staten Island; $12M.
● Restored St. Hilda's copper roofs and ornamental balustrades consistent with original design; $1.5M.
● Converted 1880 printing house into Youth Services Clinic; $1.1M.
● Named *"Architect of the Year"* by NY State Historical Society.

EMPLOYMENT

Estermand and Williams Associates   New York, NY   1990–present
Senior Architect/Restoration

C.G. Quenelles, Inc.   Fort Lee, NJ   1988–1990
Architect

Jones, Jones & Guenther   Fort Lee, NJ   1986–1988
Draftsperson

Habitat for Humanity   Various, USA   1984–1985
Workcrew member

EDUCATION

New York University   BS, Architecture, 1986

Antioch College   English major, 1982–1983

SKILLS

Proficient in *MS Word, PowerPoint, FormTool,* and *MS Publisher,* ACAD R12
Photography, Gardening
Conversant in French, Italian, and German

Licensed NY State. Member Architects Council of NYC.

Portfolio available for your review.

Pat Jones

77 Boxer Street
Cleveland, Ohio 44123
216-477-1234   Fax 216-477-1235

Qualifications: Proven effective Art Department Coordinator with 3 years' experience. Computer literate. Team-based manager.

Professional Experience:

Strategic Inc.	**Cleveland, Ohio**	**1993–present**
* Art Department Director	1994	
* Assistant Art Director	1993	

Created animation for *"Hockey Duck"* and *"VideoVision"* video games. New position of Art Department Coordinator enabled artists and programmers to eliminate time spent in preparation and set-up for graphic integration.

Versatile in using *Deluxe Animator, Autodesk Animator Pro,* and *Deluxe Paint.*

Achievements: Trained staff of 6 artists on *"Byle"* and *"Usweat"* from LucasArts
Art Coordinator on   *"Digbert Digs Out,"* 1996
"Wrath Fighters," 1995
"DoubleTrouble," 1994
Asst. Art Director on   *"Pretty Kitty,"* 1993

Compute!	**Cleveland, Ohio**	**1990–1993**
Manager/Salesperson		

Managed store averaging $17,000,000 in annual sales; initiated training classes for new computer users. Sales growth was increased from 8.6% to 11.5% per annum during tenure, while expenses decreased 1.2% due to utilization of computerized inventory program. Promoted to manager after 18 months in sales.

Education:

Cooper School of Art	Cleveland, Ohio	BA 1993
Combined art and design courses with computer graphics		
LyVelle Technical School	Cleveland, Ohio	1992
Courses in computer repair and programming		

Pat Jones
77 Boxer Street
New York, New York 10012
212-477-1234   Fax 212-477-1235
E-mail pjones@jones.com

A proven art director with a variety of experiences that include a solid reputation
for completing creative, high quality projects on time and within budgets;
over 25 years of field experience.

✦ Pat Jones ✦

PROFESSIONAL EXPERIENCE:

1981–present

Art Director   **Scully Inc.**   **Stamford, CT**

- Directly responsible for projects from concept, through all phases of design and comprehensives, to finished mechanical or final film.

- Arrange for and direct out-of-house services, including illustration, photography, film and printing for various projects.

- Direct photography sessions to ensure quality of final image.

- Pre-press and on-press supervision.

- Supervise staff of 6 designers. Responsible for annual budget of $123M in billings.

- Frequent direct contact with clients to discuss new projects, review and revise artwork. Projects include:
  - Logo design
  - Direct mail brochures
  - Sales literature
  - Package development
  - Media presentations
  - Corporate image

1980–81

Assistant Art Director   **NY, Inc.**   **New York City**

Designed and completed comprehensive roughs for brochures, logos, booklets and collateral materials, from concept to camera-ready mechanicals. Additional responsibilities included layout design, photo editing, copywriting, assistant studio and location photographer.

1978–1980

Designer   **Smith, Handy and Grives Associates**
                                               Stamford, CT

Responsible for logo, letterhead and brochure layout and design. Created paste-ups, typespecing; extensive use of stat camera and photography for in-house newsletter.

TECHNICAL SKILLS:

Extensive experience with Macintosh system and software including a thorough knowledge of drawing, scanning, word processing and page layout software:

Adobe Illustrator
Aldus FreeHand
Quark XPress
Aldus Pagemaker
Microsoft Word
Adobe Streamline
Ofoto
Adobe Photoshop

Experienced photographer; digital camera and video.

CLIENTS:

Seaman's Bank for Savings
Bank of New York
U.S. Boating Association
Evinrude
Forbes Magazine
Sunbeam Appliances

Sanibel Island Tourist Board
Ft. Meyers Chamber of Commerce
Fruit Growers Union
Marriott Corporation
Spin
NewWave Creative Artists

EDUCATION:

University of Connecticut   **Stamford, CT**
1979, BS Graphic Design with Photography Minor. Cum Laude

AFFILIATIONS:

National Designers Union   Vice President, 1995
Greenwich Village Chamber of Commerce
City Harvest, Outreach Chairperson

PORTFOLIO AVAILABLE FOR REVIEW

Pat Jones

77 Boxer Street
Cleveland, Ohio 44123
216-477-1234   Fax 216-477-1235

summary

Artist with 25 years' experience in doing murals and wall-size paintings for hotels, restaurants, and spas. Specialize in nature and environmental scenes.

work experience

Great Lakes Conservation Society
Sandusky, OH
1994–1996

Designed and completed series of murals located at visitor kiosks in 5 major lakefront cities depicting the natural wildlife found along the shore.

Captiva Chamber of Commerce
Captiva, FL
1995

Designed "Welcome Wall" Visitor's Center; coordinated supporting artwork in offices.

Tampa Shores Resort
Tampa, FL
1993

Created tiles and matching color scheme for pool and spa area.

KidsCare Corp.
Detroit, MI
1990–1993

Created series of 45 mixed-media child-focused wall paintings for chain of child-care centers.

Evergreen Inc.
Dearborn, MI
1988–1990

Designed shopping bags, hats and towels with gardening theme coordinated with mural completed at leading garden supply center.

Eat Right, Now!
Cleveland, OH
1980–1988

Painted wall-size murals at 30 sites for national chain of health food restaurants.

exhibits

Woods Art Gallery
New York, NY

1995 One-person show of nature paintings.

McWilliam School of Design Gallery
Staten Island, NY

1990 Group show *"Against the Tide"*

Cuyahoga Arts Center
Sandusky, OH

1989, 1987 Group shows

| **education** | Cooper School of Art | Cleveland, OH | BA, 1978 |

Video portfolio available for viewing upon request

PAT JONES

77 Boxer Street
New York, New York 10012
212-477-1234   Fax 212-477-1235

QUALIFICATIONS

Award-winning artist and home furnishings craftsman; work shown in galleries in Europe and New York. Specialize in maple and oak woods. Created unique lighting fixtures, cabinetry, and interiors combining practicality with tenets of classical design.

- Represented on consignment by various galleries including: in New York, Peter Rippon Gallery, Be Seated Gallery, Beverly Ann Enderly Gallery; in London, Charles & Henry Gallery and The Woodman's Way Gallery.
- Numerous exhibitions in various galleries in Europe including the Royal Academy, the Royal Festival Hall, and the Stephen Nicola Gallery in London.
- Named "Designer of the Year," 1993, Metro Magazine.

PROFESSIONAL EXPERIENCE

Pat Jones Designs
New York City
Pat Jones, Owner
1985–present

Design and cabinetry company using fine art principles and ideas to make furniture, to design and construct interiors, and to create objects and artifacts that reflect individuality but also recognize the need for practicality.

Private Commissions
1985–1996

Numerous projects and commissions including: lighting sconces for Hillside Inn, Maine; sundry furniture and cabinetry for various private residences in New York and Massachusetts; cabinetry for DeStefano Residence, New York City (featured in *The New York Times,* "Home Design," March, 1995); cabinetry for Franklin Mansion, Philadelphia; mirrors and tables for offices of the Director of *"MetroTech,"* Brooklyn, New York (through Devine Interior Designs, Inc.).

SOLO EXHIBITS

Entre Lucre Gallery
New York City

Exhibited various pieces of furniture, including tables and mirrors, 1996.

PS41 Design Space
Jersey City, New Jersey

Paintings and drawings, 1990.

Oxford Gallery
Christchurch, England

"Installations" and *"Fixtures,"* 1987. Juried show.
Awarded *First Prize.*

EDUCATION

1972–1975   **Royal Academy of Arts**, London
Post-Graduate Degree, Painting/Fine Art

1969–1972   **St. Martins School of Art**, London
B.A. Degree, Fine Art/Design

PAT JONES

77 BOXER STREET   KEY WEST, FLORIDA 33957
813-477-1234   813-477-1235/BEEPER

SUMMARY: HIGHLY-MOTIVATED, SUCCESSFUL ARTS CENTER AND MUSEUM MANAGER WITH 8 YEARS'
EXPERIENCE.
* WROTE FEDERAL GRANT THAT OBTAINED $1,750,000 IN FUNDING.
* RECRUITED AND HIRED 60 LOCAL ARTISTS TO PRESENT CREATIVE PROGRAMS.
* CREATED PROMOTIONAL PRINT AND RADIO MATERIALS.

EXPERIENCE:

DIRECTOR
BIG (BARRIER ISLAND GROUP) ARTS CENTER
KEY WEST, FLORIDA   1988–PRESENT
ESTABLISHED AND DIRECT THIS HIGHLY SUCCESSFUL PROGRAM TO PROMOTE THE ARTS TO
RESIDENTS OF ALL AGES WITHIN THE FLORIDA KEYS. ASSIST NEIGHBORING CITIES IN
ESTABLISHING SIMILAR PROGRAMS. PROMOTE EXHIBITS OF LOCAL ARTISTS.
*PRESENT THREE MAJOR EXHIBITS ANNUALLY; DEAL WITH ARTISTS & OTHER MUSEUMS
TO ARRANGE EXHIBIT. CONSULT ON HANGING OF SHOW AND PROMOTION.

*INITIATED A STATE FUNDED "ART IN OUR SCHOOLS" PROGRAM. PROGRAM STARTED IN
5 ELEMENTARY SCHOOLS AND IS EXPANDING TO 83 SCHOOLS, SEPTEMBER, 1996.

*DEVELOPED A PROFITABLE AFTERSCHOOL PROGRAM FOR HIGH SCHOOL STUDENTS AS
WELL AS WEEKEND ADULT EDUCATION; ATTENDANCE OVER 350 STUDENTS EACH
SEMESTER. PROGRAM FEATURED ON "KEYS TO LEARNING" (WEGL-TV 2/5/96).

*HIRED AND SUPERVISE OFFICE STAFF OF 10; ANNUAL BUDGET OF $2.3M.

DESIGN CONSULTANT
MIAMI ART MUSEUM
MIAMI BEACH, FLORIDA   1985–1990
CREATED ORIGINAL DESIGNS FOR COLOR, THEME, AND SPECIAL EFFECTS AT PREVIEW
PARTIES PROMOTING OPENING EXHIBITS INCLUDING: PHOTOGRAPHY OF WEEGEE, ART DECO,
MATISSE'S EARLY YEARS, AND DAVINCI'S NOTEBOOKS.

PRACTICING ARTIST   1980–PRESENT
WATERCOLORS AND ACRYLICS
WORK SHOWN IN GALLERIES IN FLORIDA, NEW YORK, AND LONDON

EDUCATION:

UNIVERSITY OF SOUTHERN FLORIDA   BA, 1982
FT. MEYERS, FLORIDA
ORGANIZED SHOW OF STUDENT WORK, 1980, 1981, 1982, 1983
MEMBER OF BOARD OF TRUSTEES

Pat Jones

77 Boxer Street   Linden, NJ 07036   908-477-1234

OBJECTIVE   Producer/Associate Producer for television network.
HIGHLIGHTS OF QUALIFICATIONS:
☆ Six years' experience in broadcast news, live show formats.
☆ Experienced in all phases of programming and production, including developing show format, research, writing & producing segments, booking guests, editing, field production.
☆ Proven ability to meet deadlines, develop creative themes and deal effectively with all members of staff and talent.

**PRODUCTION
EXPERIENCE
1995–PRESENT**   **TELEVISION HEALTHY EATING NETWORK, NEW YORK**
"GROCERIES TODAY" - Live News Magazine Show
Associate Producer
Produce, write, research, edit, and book various food, health, new products and celebrity-oriented segments for daily live show.
☆ Responsible for producing and researching taped lifestyle pieces weekly.
☆ Field produce New York and Chicago Housewares and Gourmet Food products trade shows.

1994–1995   **"DAILY FOOD VIEWS"** - Live News Show
Segment Producer
Produced, wrote, researched and booked new housewares and gourmet food products segments.
☆ Responsible for booking world's leading chefs, restaurateurs and "foodies" for daily "Live" news show.
☆ Traveling Correspondent and Field Producer for New Products Trade Shows.

1993–1994   **Production Assistant - New "Food" Cable Channel**
Part of original launch team. Researched show ideas, produced taped clips and bumpers, conducted pre-interviews of guests, assisted in booking guests and assisted with writing news copy.

1993   **CABLEVISION, WHATTADAY, NEW YORK**
Production Assistant
Prepared clips and bumpers, researched information for producers, prepared scripts, recommended story ideas, assisted in field stories.

1992–1993   **LIBERTY CABLE COMPANY, COMMUNITY BIOGRAPHIES**
Production Assistant
Gathered data, researched story ideas, wrote, produced and edited weekly lifestyles segments.

Please continue on next page

1991–1992 **WSRT RADIO STATION**
News Reporter - Host
Researched, wrote, produced and reported daily news stories and hosted the
news talk show *"Community Events This Week."*
☆ Created format and show theme, gathered information and booked guests.

EDUCATION

RUTGERS UNIVERSITY   1991
BACHELOR OF ARTS - JOURNALISM AND MASS MEDIA
☆ Produced Student Radio Broadcasts, RUTG.
☆ Summer intern ABC-TV News.
☆ Reporter & Co-editor of *Rutgers Rag,* Campus Newspaper.

SKILLS

WORD PERFECT, LOTUS 1-2-3, AP NEWS CENTER SUPERVISOR.

Pat Jones
77 Boxer Street
New York, New York 10012
212-477-1234

Objective: Position as Audio Designer for CD-ROM/Interactive division of leading computer software company.

Music Composer: Composed musical underscore for 25 educational software programs aimed at adult market.
Developed theme music for web pages for Fortune 500 clients.
Created music for commercials for NY Lottery campaign.
Arranged music for international banking division internal training films using variety of foreign traditional instruments and authentic playing techniques.

Training: Developed staff of 6 using state-of-the-art computer software programs. Instituted TQM groups to manage client projects.

Product Development: Leader of team to design and produce an interactive sound effects CD-ROM package. Brought project on-line within budget and time constraints.

Created inventory system of all instruments, scores, themes and sound effects on hand.
System resulted in annual time and cost savings of $25,000.

Musician: Piano, keyboard and synthesizer for *"Rock Fish,"* jazz-rock band.

Technical Expertise: Computer literate on PC and MAC systems with working knowledge of database and word processing. Extensive experience with audio equipment, mixing, consoles and recording devices.

Work History:

NoNet Productions, Inc.	New York, NY
Audio Composer/CD-ROM Division	1995–1996
ARKO Advertising	Jersey City, NJ
Music Composer	1994–1995
New Line Movies	Astoria, NY
Music Composer/TV Movie Unit	1994
Ritchie's Video and Laser Disc	Astoria, NY
Audio Service and Repair	1991–1994
Starlite Grill	New York, NY
Audio Technician	1991–1995

Education: UCLA   Bachelor of Arts in Music, 1994
Attended Pasadena Computer School 1991–1992

Pat Jones
77 Boxer Street
New York, New York 10012
212-477-1234   Fax 212-477-1235
E-mail pjones@jones.com

KEYWORDS: Writer, 16 years, experience, textbook, German and Italian language, translations, educational publishing, multi-media presentations, testing programs, videotape producer, MA English, BA Italian

SUMMARY: Accomplished author experienced in educational publishing on variety of topics; completes projects on time and within budget.

EXPERIENCE:

Sohm Publishing, a Division of McGraw-Hill Inc.   New York City
Author   1980–present
Wrote and revised series of high school history and social studies textbooks, student workbooks, teacher guides, audio-visual materials, and testing programs in English, German and Italian.
+ Responsible for annual review and revisions to meet needs of growing market.
+ Produce sales training materials for national sales meetings.
+ Prepare and present multi-media promotion to regional sales representatives annually.
+ Accompany sales staff on calls to promote product lines.
+ Initiated intranet service.

Integrated Language Arts   Brooklyn, NY
Publisher   1988–present
Produce videotapes and study guides for language immersion programs for corporate clients; training for executives being assigned to Germany and/or Italy.
+ Marketing and sales of videos have grown steadily (10–12% annually) since inception. Client base includes leading foreign manufacturers, financial institutions, and transportation companies.

Stuyvesant High School   New York City
Foreign Language Teacher   1980–1990
+ Initiated Italian language program.
+ Motivated numerous students to win local and national awards.
+ Involved local Italian community in support of school; annual Italian Fest celebrated student achievements and raised funds for college scholarships for further study of Italian.

EDUCATION:

Fairfield University   Fairfield, CT   MA in English, 1979
Fairfield University   Fairfield, CT   BA in Italian
+ Junior year spent studying in Rome and Florence

AFFILIATIONS:

Abba Sicula, New York chapter
Phi Beta Kappa

PAT JONES
77 BOXER STREET
ST. PETERSBURG, FLORIDA 33708
813-477-1234   Fax 813-477-1235

PROFESSIONAL PROFILE: BROADCAST JOURNALIST

Professional Experience
Television

WTTR-TV, St. Petersburg, Florida, Newscasters Inc.
Co-Anchor
1996 to Present — *"Evening News at 6:00"*
1995 to 1996 — *"News At Noon"*

WTPA-TV, Ft. Lauderdale, Florida, ABC Affiliate
On-Air Reporter
1996 to Present — *"Morning News at 5:30"*

WTSP, Tampa, Florida
Associate Producer
1994–1995 *"Good Morning Tampa Bay," "The News At Noon"*

KBSA, Everglade City, Florida,
Assignment Editor
1993–1994

Radio

WBBO 720 AM, St. Petersburg, Florida
Street Reporter
Live Wire Communications, Inc., 1994 to 1995

WNWZ 1370 AM, Hollywood, Florida
Morning Editor, Reporter, Anchor
AP Radio News, 1994 to 1995.

KBCD Headline News 860 AM, Newport News, Virginia
News Director
Shipping News Communications, Inc. 1990 to 1992;
Anchor, Reporter 1990–1991.

See next page for freelance assignments.

PAT JONES

Freelance

SUNDQUIST COMMUNICATIONS, INC., Hollywood, Florida
Journalist, Reporter, Producer
1990 to 1995
Clients included: WANT, Fort Meyers, Florida;
Radio News Service, Miami, Florida;
University of Florida KSUN,
95.5 FM, Coral Gables, Florida.

Stories have appeared on:

WINS RADIO (New York City)
KBIG (Los Angeles)
ASSOCIATED PRESS RADIO
WTMX (Chicago)

Education

Broadcast Journalism, 1989
University of Miami
Coral Gables, Florida

Pat Jones

77 Boxer Street   New York, New York 10012   212-477-1234   Fax 212-477-1235

Objective   Position as radio commercial manager and producer for national or regional clients; six years' experience as Assistant Broadcast Producer. Relocating to New York City area.

Professional Experience

San Jose Promotions, Inc.   San Jose, CA
Associate Broadcast Producer   (1990–1996)
Managed all aspects of radio commercial production for major local and national accounts including McGraw-Hill Inc., Titan Entertainment, California Air Inc., and Valley Wine Growers Association.

Provided leadership during both pre-production planning and production. Selected and coordinated directors, production houses, editors, and talent.

Supervised staff of 6; annual budget $35M.

Outstanding Programming Award, Knights of Columbus, 1995 (Journeys; WKGH)

Audio/Video Manager   (1987–1990)
Created new Audio-Video department and library. Managed all planning and day-to-day operations of in-house and subcontracted broadcast projects.

Recruited, hired, and trained staff of 3.

Administered budget of $6M; selected and purchased capital equipment in excess of $500,000.

Station WBCH   Malibu, CA
Traffic Manager   (1984–1987)
Coordinated programming with directors.

Scheduled and trafficked commercials.

Conferred with clients and representatives on availability, rates, orders, and copy.

Malibu School Board   Malibu, CA
Advertising Consultant   (1984)

Education:

UCLA, BS in Broadcast Management, 1984
Student volunteer media/promotions consultant to California political party, 1983–1984.

Pat Jones, Scribe

77 Boxer Street
Willowick, Ohio 44095

216-477-1234
Fax 216-477-1235

❧ SUMMARY ❧

Experienced professional scribe available
for private or corporate handwriting needs.
Design logos, letterhead, business cards.
- Invitations designed, envelopes addressed
- Announcements
- Posters, signs
- Unique correspondence

❧ EXPERIENCE ❧

Numerous wedding, bar/bat mitzvah invitations designed and envelopes addressed.
Birth/adoption announcements designed and addressed.

Corporate events: announcements, placecards
McGraw-Hill Author Party
Gates Corp. Annual Stockholder Meeting
Waggoner & Hills, Anniversary Celebration

Restaurant Menus
Tramps Cajun Cafe
"22"
Americana
Tavern in the Park

Film Props
Correspondence for "Emma," Vista Films
Credits for "1776," Liberty Cinema

Advertisements, Publications
The New York Times Magazine
Redbook Magazine
Yves Rocher

❧ **Sample book available for your review** ❧
Choices of styles, colors, layout … for all your special events.

Pat Jones

OBJECTIVE: Position as caterer for major hotel or resort; can relocate.

COMPETENCIES:

Caterer: Plan, organize and coordinate all phases of off-premises catering for variety of prestigious corporate clients including Chemical Bank, Tri-State Motors, Liberty Cable, Greenwich Village Chamber of Commerce.

Delivered meals for 10–1,000; theme events such as corporate anniversaries, new product promotions, retirement parties and holiday events.

Designed and executed all aspects of theme functions including flower arrangements, table settings, menu planning, food displays, and entertainment bookings.

Interview and hire wait staff of 35 servers and bartenders.

Chef: Head chef at regional award-winning restaurant specializing in Tex-Mex cuisine, 200 tables.

Sauté Chef, Pastry Chef at French-style bistro, 75 tables.

Instructor: Degree courses in Food Presentation, Restaurant Economics, Nutrition Weekend workshops on *"Cooking for Crowds."*

AWARDS: Culinary Arts Award, 1987 and 1995

Featured in Culinary Digest, Fall 1993 *"Look Who Is Cooking"*

EDUCATION: Bachelor of Culinary Arts   1986
University of Arizona   Flagstaff, Arizona

EMPLOYMENT:

Village Caterers, Inc.   New York, New York
Catering Manager   1990–present

New School for Social Research   New York, New York
Instructor, Guest Lecturer   1990–present

CYN, Inc.   Flagstaff, Arizona
Caterer   1989

Viva!   Flagstaff, Arizona
Head Chef   1987–1988

Tricolors   Flagstaff, Arizona
Sauté Chef, Pastry Chef   1984–1987

ACTIVITIES: American Culinary Guild, Charter Member since 1985
Arizona Tourist Board, Food Chairman—Special Events Committee

77 Boxer Street   New York, New York 10012   212-477-1234   Fax 212-477-1235

WINNER OF:
1st Prize
Domino Sugar
Cake-Off
1996

1st Prize
Pies and Cakes
Category
Gourmet Food
Show
1995

2nd Prize
Maison de
France Pastry
Contest
1995

Pat Jones
77 Boxer Street
Cleveland, Ohio
44001
216-477-1234

OBJECTIVE
Award-winning culinary arts student seeks position
as pastry chef in restaurant, catering establishment,
or resort. Able to relocate.
Trained in France, Societe de Gastronome with
Monsieur Gaston de Verne.

EDUCATION
Cleveland Community College, 1996
AS in Culinary Arts

Cuyahoga High School, 1993
Diploma in Culinary Arts
Work-Study Program: Food Preparation
at Patisserie Pierre

PROFESSIONAL TRAINING
Maison de France, Cleveland, Ohio 1995–1996
Courses in pastries, cakes and desserts

Travel in France, 1994
Apprentice to Monsieur de Verne,
Societe de Gastronome, Avignon, France

EMPLOYMENT
Shaker Heights Country Club
Shaker Heights, Ohio   1995–1996
Assistant Pastry Chef
Prepared desserts for parties, private events and scheduled dinners
Created the *River of Cookies*
125 tables

Guenther and Green Bakers
Eastlake, Ohio   1995
Produced high volume quality European pastries and breads

Belle-weather Café
Mentor, Ohio   1993–1994
Prepared pastries and planned dessert menu for
French-style coffee bar

Palmer Golf Club
Cleveland, Ohio   1991–1993
Waitperson in club restaurant

RELATED SKILLS
Fluent in French
MAC-computer literate

Pat Jones
77 Boxer Street
New York, New York 10012
212-477-1234   Fax 212-477-1235

Professional Accomplishments:

Specialized in coordinating environmental issues, color theory and impact on human physiology.
Pioneered a new marketing theory for Pittsburgh Art Center Visitors' Store.
Designed Student Union for University of Pittsburgh.
Selected colors for chain of suntanning salons headquartered in Pittsburgh.
Developed color scheme for logo, furnishings and accessories for major Pennsylvania architectural firm.
Taught courses in color theory at University of Pittsburgh, Graduate School
Exclusive color consultant to *Cosmetique.*

Employment History:

Couleurs de Jardin	**Paris**	**1993–1995**

Marketing and sales for major home furnishings and design house; worked closely with clients to choose and design decor for homes and offices.
Designer of wallpaper and fabric for clients and stock.
Buyer of fabric, accessories, furnishings, and paint.

DeMarco Estate	**New Haven, CT**	**1991**

Design Consultant
Renovation of private home.
Selected color theme, furnishings, fabric, paint, art and accessories.
Hired and directed contractors on-site.

Francis and Yates Inc.	**Pittsburgh, PA**	**1989–1992**

Research Associate
Conducted market research for leading research organization.

Bon Marché Department Store	**Pittsburgh, PA**	**1988–1990**

Marketing and Sales, Home Furnishings Department.

Education:

Bachelor of Arts Degree, Communication University of Pittsburgh, 1990
Continuing Education Courses in Business Management, Leadership and Marketing

Skills:

Fluent in French.   Computer literate on Macintosh systems.

Portfolio available upon request.

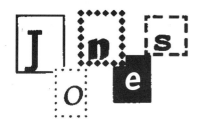

Pat Jones
77 Boxer Street   New York, New York 10012
212-477-1234   Fax 212-477-1235

WHO I AM.

Commercial artist specializing in finished illustration, known for cartoon style.
Experienced with all phases of production.

WHAT I'VE DONE.

1993–present

Liberty Advertising Agency   Brooklyn, NY
Illustration and layout for automobile, motorcycle and recreational vehicle
department.
Board work, paste-ups, comps, mechanicals and rough drafts.
Work closely with account executives and clients to develop coordinated
promotions.

 Designed *"Mr. Wheels"* character for regional car dealership; cartoon logo
for national TV promotion *"Hogs"* for Harley-Davidson; cartoon drawings
used in 1995 National Safety Board's promotion for children's seat belts.

1990–present

Freelance children's book illustrator   Chicago, IL
Responsible for the creation of the *"Flowers in My Garden"* series of nature books;
Disney's series on the history of the automobile; spot illustrations for Children's
Express Newsletter.

1978–1990

Green, White and Bloom Associates   Kansas City, MO
Created artwork from rough draft through finished pieces for various advertising
campaigns.
Developed signature cartoon style.

WHERE I STUDIED.

Kansas City School of Art   Kansas City, MO
Commercial art studied 1976–1978

THERE'S MORE ... Ask to see my book of original and printed work.

Pat Jones
77 Boxer Street
New York, New York 10012
Phone 212/477-1234
Fax   212/477-1235

❊ Qualifications ❊

•*Designed costumes for leading TV shows, music videos and films.*

•*Researched historical accuracy for period pieces.*

•*Experienced in maintaining budget and time constraints.*

•*Expert needlework and sewing skills.*

•*Prime contacts with wholesale fabric and trim shops.*

•*Skilled in working with and hiring expert staff.*

❊ Professional Experience ❊

Costume Designer
Theater of the Absurd, New York, NY
1995–present
Designed costumes for all performances
"The Merry Widow," "MacBeth's Mom," "Title XI," "The Cat With One Life"
TV special on troupe: *"On the Edge of Reason"*

Assistant Costume Designer
Scholastic Films, Hollywood, CA
1993–1995
Worked on over 25 short (30 min.) educational films distributed to children's and adult markets. Researched and designed costumes.

Costume Researcher
Nickelodeon Studios, Orlando, FL
1988–1990
Designed costumes for children's videos and TV shows; created "look" of characters in "The Big Doll House"; coordinated with franchise operators to produce stuffed animals from shows.

Assistant Costume Designer
Halloween All Year, Jersey City, NJ
1986
Created costumes in all genres for this major costume supply house; sewed and maintained costumes; maintained rental records; met with TV, Video and Film clients to discuss and plan costumes.

Freelance — various locations
1990–present
Lincoln Center Out-of-Doors, 1996
Music videos: Madonna, Cher, Billy Ray Cyrus
TV: Time Warp Jeopardy, *"Once Upon an Election"*
Film: *"Six," "Look Who's Talking 4," "Rescue"*

Costume Researcher
Acclaim Video, Hartford, CT
1991–1992
Researched costumes for historical video games; made sketches and created designs for animators to use in games.

Wardrobe Manager
New York City Opera, New York, NY
1987–1988
Kept log of all costumes; repaired and maintained condition; advised Costume Designer of need to replace; prepared all costumes in advance of each production.

Sales Clerk
Goodman's Rentals, New York, NY
1980–1985
Customer service for major costume and prop rental house; maintained records; checked costumes and props for quality; dealt with TV, Video, Theater and Film costume departments.

❊ Training ❊

Fashion Institute of Technology, New York, NY Fashion and costume design	BA, 1984
Singer Center Sewing program	1982

CREATIVE DIRECTOR/GRAPHIC DESIGN (BOOKLET FORMAT)

PAT JONES

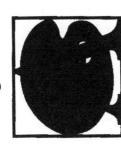

77 Boxer Street
Stamford, CT
203-477-1234   Fax 203-477-1235
E-mail pjones@jones.com

COMPETENCIES

Art Direction	Concept Development	Computer Comprehensives
Marker Comps	Brochures	Sales Promotions
Direct Mail	Package Design	Advertisements
Free-Standing Inserts	Logos	Photo Illustration
Digital Retouching	Point-of-Sale Design	Sell Sheets
Premium Design	Morphing	Letterhead Design

TECHNICAL EXPERTISE

MAC Systems
UMAX scanner/transparency adapter
Software: PhotoShop, QuarkXpress, Adobe Illustrator, Streamline, EFI Cache-Profiles, Painter

PROFESSIONAL EXPERIENCE

1994–present   Ruiz Design Studio   **Greenwich, CT**
Creative Director
Create sales promotion programs, advertising, packaging and logo designs for a $135M client base.
Supervise a team of 7 designers. Design graphics, purchase and supervise all pre-production and
production materials. Client base specializes in foreign companies seeking US consumers.

1993–1994   Williams Display Company   **Virginia Beach, VA**
Art Director
Designed ads, catalogs and brochures for men's fashions, floor coverings and housewares.

1988–1990   Gibson Card Co.   **Cleveland, OH**
Artist/ Holiday Card Division
Designed Christmas, Easter, and Valentine's Day cards.

EDUCATION

Cooper School of Art, BFA, 1990   **Cleveland, OH**
Courses in computer graphics at The New School, NY

ACHIEVEMENTS

1995   MTV Achievement Awards Show   Designed programs, graphics
1994   Lincoln Center Out of Doors   Created poster, image for series
1993   Cooper School of Art   Designed new logo, letterhead and catalog layout
1991   Cleveland Institute of Art   Developed theme in signs, posters and
                                         brochures for "Modern Egypt"

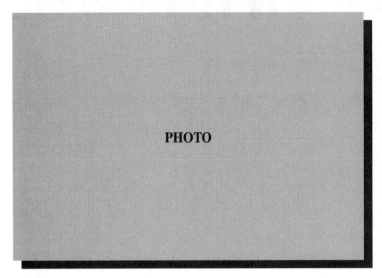

Height: 5′8″

Weight: 108 lbs.

Eyes: Blue

Hair: Auburn

Voice: Alto

Pat Jones
Dancer•choreographer•singer

•PROFESSIONAL EXPERIENCE

McGREGOR DANCE TROUPE Washington, DC
Dancer / Choreographer
(Feb 89 to present)
Travel extensively throughout the region performing for children, senior citizens, and disabled audiences.

Write 2 original dances each year: spring and winter performances.

Developed special program to include disabled performers for benefit show.

Headliner at the American Cancer Society annual conference.

DISNEYWORLD Orlando, FL
Tap Your Feet
(Aug 88 to Jan 89)
Lead dancer; 6 performances weekly for run of show.

AVERY FISHER HALL New York City, NY
Peace Whirls (Jul 88)
Dancer; special performance for United Nations Celebration.

UNITED STATES DANCE INTERNATIONAL Miami, FL
Dancer (Dec 86 to Jun 88)
Member dance troupe.
Performed American period, popular, and musical theater dance on cruise ships.
Performed in holiday jazz concert with the Tampa Symphony Orchestra.

•TELEVISION EXPERIENCE

UNIVERSAL STUDIOS Los Angeles, CA
Commercial shoot for 1996 promotion, NIKE SPORTS
WFGY   Cleveland, OH   **History of Jazz, 1993**
F/X TV   New York, NY   **Fashions, 1991**

Performances available on video for your review

77 Boxer Street   Brooklyn, NY 11256   718-477-1234

Pat Jones
77 Boxer Street
Palo Alto, CA 94306
415.477.1234
http:/www.pjones.com

KEYWORDS: art, multi-media, design, Adobe Photoshop + Strata StudioPro + Macromedia Director +Xaos Pandemonium Alias v7 + Adobe Illustrator + Autodesk 3D Studio +Xaostitle +Quark Xpress, team player, cover art, CD-ROM, video games, 3D, toy industry, digital illustration, digital artist, animator, catalog, POP displays, marketing.

OBJECTIVE
A position in electronic art multi-media and design.

SKILLS
Proficient in the following graphics, multi-media and publishing applications:
Adobe Photoshop + Strata StudioPro + Macromedia Director +Xaos Pandemonium Alias v7 + Adobe Illustrator + Autodesk 3D Studio +Xaostitle +Quark Xpress

EMPLOYMENT HISTORY
1995–PRESENT
Present freelance clients include:

TIME WARNER TOYS INC. So. San Francisco CA
Digital design and development illustrations for one of the largest toy manufacturers in the nation. By using Studio Pro Photoshop and Illustrator I provided conceptual artwork for line of WCW Wrestlers NWO and Sabrina Teen Witch figures. Creating detailed 3-D models from simple line drawings and schematics, I worked closely with the development staff to help bring their ideas to light.

READER'S DIGEST INTERACTIVE
Cover Illustration for BOOK WORM, a game for the Sony Playstation.

NINTENDO
Digital illustrations and design for SUPER MARIO games' packaging. Using Studio Pro and Photoshop I create detailed artwork that reflects the enhanced graphics running in the current generation of home game systems.

ATARI
Product developer and graphic artist in the toy division where I was responsible for =REALIZING= concepts as well as further developing existing product designs by using 3-D modeling programs and animation including the modeling of 3-D environments. Attended classes in Autodesk 3-D Studio sponsored by SEGA as well as producing artwork and design for interactive children's books and comics.

1993–95
MILTON-BRADLEY San Jose CA
Illustrated technical manuals for various online UNIX-based software applications.

1992–93
STARTER, INC. Monte Sereno CA
Designed and produced all promotional material for the 94 season.
Worked closely with VP to create a graphic identity for the teams logo

1992
INTUIT, INC. Palo Alto CA
Designed SPC mailers for QUICKEN campaign.
Produced marketing materials.
Package design including cover illustration for QUICKEN.

1992
OZ-JUDY JUICE COMPANY So. San Francisco CA
Produced 3-D illustrations for marketing.
Designed POP displays for all Shop-Rite stores.
Created ads for newsprint.

1992
H-P SOLUTIONS Burlingame CA
Designed a ten-page catalog.
Worked one-on-one with marketing director.

EDUCATION
Academy of Art College San Francisco CA
BA, Design, 1994
Deangelis Community College Cupertino CA
AS degree in computer generated art and design, 1992

PAT JONES
77 Boxer Street
New York, New York 10012
212-477-1234   Fax 212-477-1235

OBJECTIVE_____
Seasoned professional with 25 years' experience in entertainment production seeking to relocate to tri-state area.

PROFESSIONAL SUMMARY_____
Manager with over 7 years' experience in development and operation of entertainment productions and special events.

> Demonstrated ability to effectively motivate and manage personnel, develop contracts and conduct negotiations, produce programs and special events including budgeting, scheduling, hiring and directing.

> Broad range of management expertise coupled with creative skills.

MAJOR ACCOMPLISHMENTS_____
Entertainment Production

> Designed staging areas and types of entertainment appropriate for each, including daily parades and special events.

> Worked with consulates and embassies around the world, resulting in entertainment productions by nearly 100 international groups and individuals.

> Designed and implemented program to recruit quality non-professional groups such as college and high school bands for daily parades, resulting in over 800 such groups from around the U.S.

> Auditioned, hired and managed all on-site and/or shipboard entertainment including musical shows, cabaret, variety, costume characters, street performers, international groups, non-professional groups.

Management

> Managed all aspects of entertainment productions and individual entertainers at up to ten simultaneous venues and with up to 200 entertainers.

> Directed hiring, training and management of over 100 part-time representatives along with office employees, including development of written training materials.

Administration

> Administered all contract negotiations, transportation, lodging, etc. for hundreds of on-site and ship-board contract and employee entertainers and entertainment groups.

> Developed and monitored departmental budgets for world's largest cruise line, world's fair, theme park, dance company and personally owned companies, always maintaining costs at or below budget.

> Conducted feasibility and profitability studies for property acquisition and rezoning, resulting in gains of up to fifty percent in property values.

> Created short and long term business plans and accompanying budgets and personnel requirements for both entertainment and service related projects.

continued

EMPLOYMENT HISTORY

Manatee State Arts Company (Punta Gorda, FL) Executive Director	1994 to Present
Jones, Inc. (Coral Gables, FL) President/Owner	1990–1994
Florida Realty International, Inc. Vice President - Acquisitions	1985–1989
Brookhaven Management Co. (Tampa, FL) Manager of Corporate Marketing	1984–1985
Carnival Cruise Lines Director of Entertainment	1983–1984
Cedar Point Theme Park (Sandusky, OH) Entertainment Director	1982–1983
The 1982 World's Fair (Corporate offices) On-site Entertainment Manager	1980–1982
Williamsburg/Busch Gardens Attractions Manager	1979–1980

EDUCATION

Graduate studies	University of Toronto Marketing, 1979
Bachelor of Arts	Cleveland State University English, Cum Laude, 1975

Pat Jones

77 Boxer Street   New York, New York 10012   212-477-1234   Fax 212-477-1235

Summary

Dynamic public events planner with over 10 years' experience creating,
promoting, organizing major events in the tri-state area.
- Media preparations for Pope John Paul II visit.
- Planned and implemented media coverage and logistics for
NY Rangers Stanley Cup celebration on Broadway.
- Initiated annual *"Spring Fling"* city-wide celebration of the advent of spring.

Professional Experience

What's Happening Now, Inc.
President and Founder
Jersey City, NJ 1987 to present

Public Relations firm specializing in large-scale public special events

Originated and organized all facets of the annual March celebration "Spring Fling,"
with a current staff of 125 and 200 volunteers; budget of $250,000. Participation in
this event has grown from 2,000 (1991) to 35,000 (1996).

Promoted and planned logistics for special events such as *You Gotta Have Park,*
Washington Square Outdoor Concert series,
Panasonic Jazz Fest, Battery Park Dragon Boat Races.

Organized fund-raising and public service events such as
Health Week `95, *Race for the Cure, Athletes Against Aids (AAA)*
and *Get the Vote Out `92.*

WCVG-TV's *"THE ART IN YOU"*
Director
Dayton, Ohio 1985–1987
Weekly hour-long television program showcasing local talent.

UNITED WRESTLING CORP.
Director of Special Events
Stamford, CT 1983–1985
Assisted in the development and coordination of ticket promotions, give-away campaigns,
college nights, retirement ceremonies, old timers night, and clinics.

EDUCATION

B.A. in Marketing   Ohio State University, 1983

AFFILIATIONS

Marketing Managers Association, President
Jersey City Chamber of Commerce

Pat Jones

77 Boxer Street
Albany, New York 90012
532-477-1234
Cell 532-477-1235

CAREER OBJECTIVE

Senior executive position coordinating fashion displays, purchasing and promotion with a major department store specializing in women's high quality fashions.

QUALIFICATIONS

Fashion expert with over 25 years' experience, last 10 years with major department store.

Coordinated with buyers, window dressers, marketing and sales staff.

Arranged seasonal fashion shows and promotions.

Developed cross-selling product tie-ins.

Scheduled celebrity fashion shoots.

EDUCATION

Duke University	1966–1970
Major:	Advertising (Business Administration)
Minor:	Applied Arts
SKILLS	Fluent in Italian; conversant in Spanish
AFFILIATIONS	Art League Abba Sicula Albany Fashion Institute Advisory Board ItalianTravel Council

EMPLOYMENT

1986–1996
Keystone Department Store, Albany, NY
Fashion Coordinator for main store and 3 mall outlets. Created unified "look" for all the stores, coordinating store decorations and shopping bag design.

Established Keystone as a prime sales point for leading Italian knitwear designers; initiated "Festa Italia" to highlight designers which accounts for 10% of annual women's fashion sales.

Hosted "Young Designers" Showcase to develop local student talent from Albany Fashion Institute.

Hired, trained, supervised staff of 7 "Professional Shoppers," new service started in 1990 which accounted for 8% of net profits 1995.

(Keystone Department Store closed due to fire, September 1996.)

1976–1977
Benderetta's, Houston, TX
Co-owner bridal shop. Ordered stock, fitted dresses and did window displays. Responsible for advertising and annual Bridal Show.

1974–1976
A++ Models, Philadelphia, PA
High Fashion Print Model

1972–1974
WJW - TV, Washington, DC
Weather reporter, television commercials

Prior to 1972
Freelance photo modeling (London, Paris, Canada, USA)

AWARDS/ACCOMPLISHMENTS

Civic Award, Albany B.I.D. 1992
Host "Bridal News," MTV Fashion Awards 1989
Spokesperson, Italian Export Guild, 1976–1977

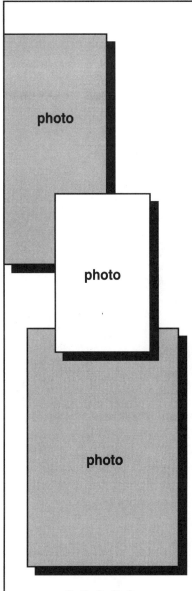

Pat Jones
77 Boxer Street
New York, New York 10012
212-477-1234
Fax 212-477-1235

Summary: Figure skating instructor with 20 years' experience competing and teaching; group and private lessons; featured performer national ice show.

Experience:

Chelsea Skating School
New York, NY
❆ Instructor
1990–present

Teach classes in basic technique, intermediate and advanced levels.

Group lessons for up to 15 students. Coached Mid-Atlantic Junior Champion, 1994.

City Nights Ice Dancers
New York, NY
❆ Figure Skater/Ice Dancer
1994–present

Performer with local ice show, *Broadway on Ice*; featured solo "Evita." National tour, Summer 1995.

Education: Mount Manhattan College BA, 1984

Training: Dance, with Olga Wilders
Skating, with Damian Reives (1982–86); with Preston Quinn (1973–82)

Skills: Dance — Ballet, Jazz, Modern
Trampoline, Gymnastics, Piano, Guitar

Performance tapes available.

❆❆❆❆❆❆

North-East Regional Champion, 1990, 1986; Second-place, 1983

Vermont Open Competition Champion, 1980

Mid-Atlantic Juniors Champion, 1977

Pat Jones

77 Boxer Street
New York, New York 10012
212-477-1234   Fax 212-477-1235
E-mail pjones@jones.com

---- ---- ---- ---- ---- ---- ---- ---- ---- ----

····FILM EDITING·CAMERA·PRODUCTION·DIRECTION·SPECIAL F/X····

---- ---- ---- ---- ---- ---- ---- ---- ---- ----

PROFESSIONAL EXPERIENCE:
Down Pat Productions
Freelance Film and Video Producer   *1987 to present*

Directed a full-length nature film previewed at the National Historical Society (1996). Responsible for camera work and editing.

Produced a "70's sci-fi film" previewed on WPLJ's Graveyard Shift. Responsible for writing, camera work, directing, and editing.

Produced an 8mm video of above film previewed at Tisch Art School. Responsible for writing, camera work, directing, and editing.

Corporate/commercial clients include:

Sunbeam Bread	*GNC Stores*
Acer Technology	*Jazzmix Arts*
Tribeca Films	*Paper Access*

Freelance Musician   *1980 to present*

Flutist with area jazz bands. Record commercials and sound tracks, *"Sounds of Eire"* CD (1996), *"Irish Spring"* commercial (1996), Medieval Times restaurant commercial (1995).

Radio Personality   *1985 to 1987*
KOKL Omaha, NE
D.J. and talk show host for a news radio station.

TRAINING:

16mm Film Production - 16mm Film Editing	New York Film Works
Video Production - Super 8 Film Production	Tisch Film Institute
Video Production - Special Effects	Cleveland Art Institute
Super 8 Production, Editing and Sound	Sound & Vision Screenings

EDUCATION:

A.S. in **Communications**   1985
UCLA   Los Angeles, CA

Pat Jones

77 Boxer Street
New York, New York 10012
212-477-1234
Fax 212-477-1235

Golf Pro

❖ USPGA-certified golf teaching professional.
❖ Successful experience in commissioned sales of golf instruction.
❖ Strong background in program assessment, development, and implementation.
❖ Outstanding interpersonal and motivational skills with students at all levels.

Employment Highlights:

HEAD TEACHING PRO

Sanctuary Golf Club Sanibel, FL   1989 to present

❖ Personally execute a capacity schedule of lessons on a commissioned basis.

❖ Generate a core of repeat students through expansion of instructional programs; registration has increased 35% over past 2 years.

❖ Participate in intra-club promotions to increase membership and participation.

❖ Spearheaded 4 teams to Divisional wins and advancement within the League.

❖ Network with manufacturers of athletic equipment and clothing.

❖ Select quality equipment and clothing for sale in the pro shop.

CO-HEAD TEACHING PRO

Fort Myers Country Club Fort Meyers, FL   1987 to 1989

ASSISTANT TEACHING PRO

Naples Golf Club Naples, FL   Summers 1985 and 1986

Golf Achievements:

❖ No. 1 RANKING, 1987
Mid-Atlantic Amateur Golf Association

❖ WINNER, 1986
Mid-Atlantic Sectional Amateur Golf Championships

❖ WINNER, 1985
South Carolina Amateur Golf Championships

Education:

A.S. IN BUSINESS, 1987
Briggs University Columbia, SC

Pat Jones

77 Boxer Street
Euclid, Ohio 44123
216-477-1234

Objective

To obtain a position in a graphic arts or design firm.
- Experienced in TV, 3D Graphics.
- Able to meet deadlines and budgets for client promotions.

Education

B.S. IN GRAPHIC COMMUNICATIONS

Cleveland State University   Cleveland, Ohio   1996

➤ Public Relations concentration.
➤ Who's Who in American Colleges and Universities.
➤ Dean's List, Honor Society, and Outstanding Academic Award.
➤ Public Relations Director, University NewsNotes.
➤ Class Valedictorian.

Work Experience

INTERN / GRAPHICS DEPARTMENT

KSTV - Willowick, Ohio
1993 to 1996

Prepare television graphics for nightly news program.

INTERN / PRODUCTION OFFICE

KSTV - Euclid, Ohio
1991 to 1993

Personally assisted Producer of popular weekly talk show.

GRAPHIC DESIGNER

P & S Graphics - Eastlake, Ohio
1990 to 1991

Created original graphic designs for product merchandising.
Projects included logos, packaging designs, point-of-purchase
displays, and promotional literature.

Additional Expertise

Pen & Ink Drawing, Charcoal Renderings
Corel Print House, Corel FLOW, Corel PHOTO-PAINT,
Corel Motion 3D & Corel PRESENTS

Pat Jones

77 Boxer Street
New York, New York 10012
212-477-1234   Fax 212-477-1235
E-mail pjones@jones.com

QUALIFICATIONS:

* Master of Fine Arts majoring in Graphic Design.
* Proven ability to understand client concerns and meet deadlines.
* Accomplished at interacting with clients and production personnel.
* Expert at integrating design, production, sales, and marketing considerations.
* Manage large-scale graphic promotion projects and remain within budget.

PROFESSIONAL EXPERIENCE:

Freelance Designer (1989 to present)
DRAKE GRAPHICS - Fort Lee, NJ

Supervise design projects including direct mailers, trade show graphics, mastheads, slides, catalogs, and newsletters from concept through final production.

Expert at layout, design, type specification, copy fitting, paste-up, procurement of photographs, and supervision of final printing.

Key accounts include Duckhead Publishing, Burlington Office Systems, Blue Sky Publishing Company, DataSafe Information Services, and College Town Press.

Art Director (1985 to 1989)
FORT LEE ADVERTISING AGENCY - Newport, NJ

Directed Graphic Arts staff in the creation of hard-hitting advertisements for trade journals and glossy magazines. Agency won numerous design awards.

Assistant Art Director (1983 to 1985)
NOYES CORPORATION - New York, NY

TECHNICAL SKILLS:

OmniPage Pro, OmniForm, Visio Technical, CorelDraw, FreeHand Graphics Studio, Photoshop, PageMaker, Powerpoint, Word, Nikon Scantouch, Corel Web Designer, Visual C++

EDUCATION:

MFA In Graphic Design (1983)
BFA In Graphic Design (1981)
TRAVIS SCHOOL OF DESIGN - Brooklyn, NY

Work samples on website http:/www.grafix/jones.com

From: gantor.core.com/marat Mon Sep 29 08:31:52 1996
Date: Mon. 29 Sep 1996 08:55:44 -0400
From: jones@gator.pipeline.com
Subject: Graphic Design in NYC

Pat Jones
77 Boxer Street
New York, New York 10012
212-477-1234 Fax 212-477-1235
E-mail pjones@jones.com

OBJECTIVE: Seeking a graphic design position/internship in NYC for the summer.

EDUCATION: School of Visual Arts, NYC
             Bachelor of Fine Arts, Graphic Design,
             expected May 1997
             Academic Scholarship Award

COMPUTER
PROGRAMS: Quark XPress 3.3.1
             Adobe Photoshop 3.0.5
             Adobe Illustrator 6.0
             Director 4.0.4
             ClarisWorks

SKILLS:

             Corporate Identity   Letterheads
             Packaging Design   Business Cards
             Creative Logo Design   Toy Design
             Typography   Textile Design
             Illustration   Painting
             CD Covers   Advertisements

EXPERIENCE:

             Erte's Design Studio, NYC   Summer 1995
             Designed various logos.

             Management Graphics, NYC   Spring 1995
             Created business letterheads and stationery.

Pat Jones
77 Boxer Street
New York, New York 10012
212-477-1234

OBJECTIVE: Position with film, theater or television production company; freelance.
- ▸ Experienced with male and female hair fashions.
- ▸ Extensive research done on fashion history.
- ▸ Create new and unusual hair designs for "futuristic" looks.
- ▸ Specialty: new age or punk "do's," hair wraps, braids.

EMPLOYMENT HISTORY:

Club Productions, New York   **1995–present**
Music video productions.

Prince	"Hot New Car"	Willy Smith
The Cars	"Ride With You?"	Spike Jones
Rusted Root	"Get Down"	Ellen Travis
Smashed Grapes	"Whatever"	Laurel D.

NBC Television, New York   **1993–1995**
"What the World Will Do" Daytime soap
Head hair stylist for all characters; series had dream sequence back in time to early 1700's. Researched and styled hair for historical accuracy.

Barnum & Bailey's Circus, Orlando, FL   **1991–1993**
Traveled domestically and internationally with circus troupe. Responsible for hair styles of dancers, performers. Fantasy show: "2001" required futuristic looks. Also styled wigs.

Bloomingdale's Hair Salon, New York   **1992**
Cut, styled, colored clients' hair; adult and children; unisex.

Clairol Color Labs, New York   **1991**
Cut, colored and styled volunteers' hair; specialized in temporary color treatments.

TRAINING:

Technical Hair Institute, New York   **1990–1991**
Certificate in Hair Care

L'Oreal Color Institute   **1989**
Program in hair coloring and styling

Pat Jones

**77 Boxer Street
Denver, Colorado
99001
303-477-1234
303-477-1235 Fax**

WINTERS UNIVERSITY
Denver, CO 1990

Concierge
SHERATON HOTEL
Denver, CO
May 1990 to present

Assistant Functions
Coordinator
STEAM BOAT LODGE
Steamboat Springs, CO
May 1989 to May 1990

Night Manager
HIGH POINT
RESTAURANT
Denver, CO
May 1988 to May 1989

OBJECTIVE:

Concierge for a large, metropolitan hotel. Experienced in all phases of public relations and customer service. Willing to relocate.

EDUCATION:

Bachelor of Arts in Hotel Management
Concentration in Public Relations
American Marketing Association Scholar

RELATED EXPERIENCE:

• Successfully perform all responsibilities related to this position including staff coordination, customer service and public relations.

• Closely collaborate with all departments to ensure smooth hotel operations and the implementation of special programs.

• Received outstanding performance evaluations in the areas of job knowledge, dependability, resourcefulness, and overall professionalism.

• Performed as Host at Annual Talent Show.

• Supported Function Manager in all areas of planning and supervising small and large (up to 1000 attendees) group functions.

• 500 room lodge and ski resort operates year-round

• 250 seat upscale fine dining establishment

• Responsible for staffing, food ordering and customer service.

SKILLS:

· PC-literate; MSWord, QuickBooks, Excel and Access.
· Conversant in French.

Pat Jones
77 Boxer Street
New York, New York 10012
212-477-1234

OBJECTIVE

Position in interior design firm.
•Owned and operated French antique shop for over 25 years, excellent management and sales skills.
•Extensive professional contacts in southern France and the Riviera.
•Fabric designer with nearly 10 years' experience in home furnishings; 25 years' experience importing fabric.

PROFESSIONAL
HISTORY

Jones Antique Exports, Inc., Paris, France. 1970–1996
Pat Jones, Proprietor

Antique importing business, dealing mostly with 18th- and 19th-century furniture. Imported fabric from Italy and Spain.
Provided shopping service for clients interested in redecorating residences.

Handled all import/export documentation and licenses. Dealt with government agencies and trade unions. Hired and supervised staff of 6.

Recently sold business because of desire to return to U.S.

Carlton Furniture Co., New York City 1961–1970
Fabric designer for upholstery, draperies, slipcovers and other home furnishings.

PROFESSIONAL MEMBERSHIPS

American Society of Interior Designers, since 1969
Societé de Fabrique, since 1972

EDUCATION

B.A., Rhode Island School of Design 1960
Interior design and fabric design

Lycee Americain Paris 1972-1974
Studied French language and culture

SPECIAL SKILLS

Fluent in French and Italian
Carpentry and framing

JEWELRY DESIGNER (FREELANCER, BROCHURE FORMAT)

Pat Jones

77 Boxer Street
Middlebury, RI 99578
800-477-1234
Fax 800-477-1235

Professional Experience:

Metalsmith
DESIGNS BY CHRISTINE, INC.
Newport, RI (1985 to present)
14k gold, sterling silver jewelry

Potter & Metalsmith
UNDER THE SEA
Newport, RI (1983 to 1985)
Porcelain, sterling silver

Pottery Instructor
COMMUNITY CENTER
Cranston, RI (1981 to 1983)

Metalsmith
JEWELS FOR ALL
Providence, RI (1978 to 1985)
Sterling silver, 14k gold jewelry

Fine Arts Teacher
ST. TITAN'S HIGH SCHOOL
Providence, RI (1979 to 1985)

Studio Arts Teacher
PROVIDENCE HIGH SCHOOL
Providence, RI (1977 to 1978)
PROVIDENCE CRAFT CENTER
Providence, RI (1987)
Stone Setting (Instructor. Ned Ames)

Education:

STATE UNIVERSITY OF NEW YORK
New Paltz, NY (1976)
Bachelor of Arts cum laude

WENTWORTH MUSEUM SCHOOL
Providence, RI (1986)
Metalsmithing & Ceramics

TREMBLAY SCHOOL OF CRAFT
Pawtucket, RI (1985)
Jewelry

Galleries:

Rhode Island Crafts
Newport, RI (1989,1991)
Artful Crafts II & III Exhibits

Jeweled Box
Newport, RI (1985 to present)
Juried Exhibitor

Newport Art Association
Newport, RI (1989,1990,1991)
Stones, Gems and Gold (Juried)

Society of Arts and Crafts
Boston, MA (1987 to present)

Gallery of Jewels
Pawtucket, RI (1991)
Featured Artist

Society of Arts and Crafts
Providence, RI (1 988 to 1990)
Juried Exhibitor

Truman Boutique
Newport, RI (1990,1991)
One-Person Show

Professional Associations:

Society of Goldsmiths
Providence, RI (1983 to present)

Arts Americana
Providence, RI (1988 to present)

National Crafts Council
New York, NY (1982 to present)

Museum of Artisans
New York, NY (1986 to present)

American Arts Foundation
New York, NY (1980 to present)

Pat **J**ones
77 Boxer Street
New York, New York 10012
212-477-1234
FAX 212-477-1235

Objective-   Senior design position with entertainment or lighting/audio organization.

◆Handle component and system-level repair and testing of lighting and audio equipment.

◆Assist in planning and implementation of audio and lighting systems, as well as job scheduling.

◆Train and supervise personnel in effective work procedures.

Employment-
1991–present   **Fever Lights and Sound, Inc.**   **Woodside, NY**
Lighting Technician Foreman
Supervise field installation team.
Responsible for installing, servicing, and maintaining stage lighting at major events, such as *Papal Mass at Giants' Stadium*
Woodstock 2
Diana Ross Concert in Central Park
Three Tenors in Concert at the Meadowlands

1989–present   **PJ Productions**   **NY, NY**
Lighting Designer *freelance*
Design lighting for various shows on and off Broadway. Supervise stage crews and lighting board operators, produce cue sheets, and assist the production staff in planning and implementation of lighting systems.

◆Recent Clients: *DANCE'96* AT LINCOLN CENTER
COWGIRLS
YANKEE OLD-TIMERS' GAME CELEBRATION
MADISON *SCARE* GARDEN HALLOWEEN

1990–present   **Second Stage Productions**   **NY, NY**
Audio Technician
Coordinate various events for groups, bands, churches, and production companies. Responsible for installing, servicing, and maintaining all audio equipment.

◆Recent Clients: *City Hall*   *NYPD Blue*
Caroline in the City *JazzFest '96*
1996 MTV Music Awards/KISS Remote
"One Night," Times Square 12/31/1995

Continued

1974–1988   **U.S. Navy/ West Germany
Communications/Technology Spec. 6**

Training-

Volt & Holt   EWL, West Germany   1988
Completed 200 hours of electronics

Vashon Technology Inc.   Sunnydale, CA   1987
General Electrical

Education-

Graduate U.S. Naval Communications Training
Fort Gordon, GA   1975

Thomas A. Edison Voc. & Tech HS   1974

Pat Jones

OBJECTIVE Using my photographer's background, knowledge of the area, and professional "eye" to obtain a position with a film company as a location scout.

Recent projects include:

New Line Cinema	*Sabrina Teen Witch*
MultiMedia Inc.	*CyberCom*
AT & T	Commercials
Sega	Commercials
MGM	*Die? Hardly!*
NYPD Blue	Series; 4 segments

EMPLOYMENT HISTORY

1992–1995 **Location Scout and Location Manager.**
Worked for various commercial, television, and feature production companies in New York City, Detroit, Chicago, Las Vegas and Los Angeles.

Researched, surveyed, secured and managed filming locations in a variety of urban, suburban and country environments.

1989–1991 **Freelance Photographer.**
Worked with architects, interior designers, site-planners and landscape architects in New York, Connecticut and New Jersey documenting projects for portfolios and advertising.

1986–1987 **Assistant Photographer,** Thorne Photography, Boston, MA Commercial still-photography studio.
Arranged merchandise for product photography.
Prepared configurations of 4x5 inch, 3.25 inch and 35mm format cameras using Speedotron lighting packages.

Served as on-site darkroom technician, for color and black & white photographs

EDUCATION

1988–1991 **Virginia Commonwealth University,** Richmond, VA
B.F.A., *cum laude,* Communication Arts and Design.

1987–1988 **L'accademia di Bel'Arte di Macerata,** Macerata, Italy
Visiting Scholar; photography

1984–1986 **The North Carolina School of the Arts,** Winston-Salem, N.C.
High school diploma with specialization in the visual arts and photography.

ADDITIONAL SKILLS Fluent in Italian.

77 Boxer Street New York, New York 10012 212-477-1234 Fax 212-477-1235

Pat Jones
77 Boxer Street
Brooklyn, NY 11215
h (718) 477-1234 w (212) 477-3732

Professional Goals: To work as a multimedia developer, content-oriented website designer or with on-line publishing

Related Experience:

Webmaster for the English and Comparative Literature Department at Columbia University, a cable TV show and a Massachusetts network for battered women; trained department staff in HTML and developed Web page manual for departmental use.

Currently working on a site for "The Works," a NYC modern dance company and an international fall conference at Columbia. Coursework in advanced Web Site design at Columbia and the New York Foundation for the Arts. Personal Web site mentioned in the June 1996 issues of Curve and Time Out New York.

>*Intern, I-Magic Multimedia Awards Festival, June 1996

>*Departmental representative, Interdepartmental Committee on Academic Information (Computer) Systems

Additional Skills:

HTML, familiarity with CGI scripts, learning JAVA. Adobe PhotoShop, Quark Xpress, PageMaker, CorelDraw, CorelVentura; WordPerfect 6.0 for DOS and Windows, Microsoft Word, Microsoft Excel; versatility with Macs and PCs, type 85 wpm; black-and-white photography, training in shooting and editing video and film; some knowledge of Spanish.

Education:

M.A. in English Literature (Cultural Studies emphasis),
Columbia University, May 1996.
Thesis "Staging the Nation: Sub-Nationalism on the World Wide Web"

Radcliffe Publishing Course certificate, August 1989
B.A. in English Literature, Grinnell College, May 1989

Current Employment:

Ph.D. Coordinator, English and Comparative Literature Department, Columbia University. January 1994 - present. Responsible for design and maintenance of the English Department Web page, implemented and currently administer seven e-mail lists for graduate students/ department administration.

Adviser and administrative coordinator for 300 Master of Philosophy/Ph.D. students; schedule oral examinations, review students' progress; assist the Chair and the Directors of Graduate Studies.

Employment History:

Administrative assistant, East Asian Institute, Columbia University. August 1993–January 1994. Administratively supported four Institute professors with correspondence, maintained course files and syllabi, placed book orders, organized reserve readings, assembled course packets.

Graduate Coordinator, Anthropology Department, Columbia University. January–August 1993. Initiated a database program for graduate student records. Advised 150 students in the M.A. and M.A./Ph.D. programs, scheduled certifying examinations, maintained records of student progress, certified candidates for M.A., M.Phil. and Ph.D. degrees.

Administrative assistant, Paul Smith, New York City. Sept. 1990–Jan. 1993 Children's book buyer, Spring Street Books, New York City. Aug. 1990–Jan. 1991 Editorial assistant, Farrar Straus & Giroux children's books, Aug. 1989–May 1990

Visit Websites to see my work:
    http:/www.exacta.com
    http:/www.edu.cu/pjones.com
    http:columbia.3478.com

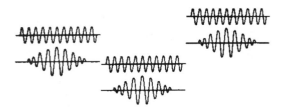

PAT JONES
77 Boxer Street
Englewood, NJ 07631
(201) 477-1234
Internet Address: pjones@jones.com

OBJECTIVE: *To secure a leadership position in project management within a company that requires the benefits of today's interactive, new media environment.*

PROFESSIONAL EXPERIENCE:

The Multimedia Publishers Bureau Princeton, New Jersey
Producer (1995 to Present)

Created and staffed new multimedia division to expand product line. Licensed programming, video, and MPEG encoding equipment (hardware and software) to minimize vendor costs. Obtained high-return program content. Identify and develop revenue generating, low risk business opportunities with local, national, and international organizations. Design, develop, and demonstrate additional product prototypes in response to customer requests.

Proactive Systems, Inc.   Newark, New Jersey
Project Manager (1992–1994)
Provided leadership to product managers for quality, budgetary, timeline, content, and overall presentation issues, to establish consistency in product development. Researched, evaluated, and implemented new technologies to enable the organization to offer state of the art new media services at competitive prices. Produced and directed educational and promotional interactive programming that always met or exceeded original objectives on time and within budget.

21st Century Visuals Inc.   Jersey City, New Jersey
Production Manager (1988–1992)
Managed projects for medical conferences, conventions, and symposia. Delegated activities of in-house and freelance personnel so that program deadlines could be met. Prepared program budgets. Selected and directed remote production facilities' activities.

EDUCATION & PROFESSIONAL AFFILIATIONS

Multi-Media Professionals Group   Executive Board Member   Hillside, New Jersey

New York University, Stern School of Business
MBA Program   Major, Management

Rochester Institute of Technology   New York
B.S. Television/Radio Communications

Pat Jones
77 Boxer Street New York, New York 10012
212-477-1234   Fax 212-477-1235
E-mail pjones@jones.com

SUMMARY   Producer with extensive CD-ROM experience.
Comprehensive working knowledge of all phases of production.
Strong communication, leadership and team coordination skills.
Innovative writer of fiction, non-fiction and interactive materials.

COMPETENCIES

Production
❖Coordinated 18 member team of creative professionals, including artists, musicians and writers.
❖Responsible for game design, script writing, asset and database management, art and audio processing, bug testing.
❖Researched content, assisted in production, videotaping and photographing on location.
❖Arranged for the acquisition of stock footage and locations for filming of multimedia science curriculum for classroom-based interactive learning.
❖Assisted in production of CD-1, Macintosh and PC discs, Nintendo Cartridges and Prodigy games.

Design
❖Designed and developed interactive educational CD-ROMs and Sega Cartridges.
❖Worked in conjunction with AppleWorks to plan interface design of virtual reality visits to the seashore and the forest.

Writing
❖Wrote interactive dialogue for *Science Kids* CD-ROM products.
❖Wrote reviews of WWW sites for *Kids' Net Guide.*
❖Created games, wrote stories and designed activities for *Sports Time* on Prodigy.

Continued ...

PROFESSIONAL EXPERIENCE

PIPELINE CORPORATION, New York, NY
1996–Present
Freelance Writer

NICKEL & DIME PRODUCTIONS, New York, NY
1991–1995
Interactive Technologies Division

❖Writer   *August 1995–December 1995*
❖Associate Project Manager   *March 1995–June 1995*
❖Associate Producer   *April 1994–March 1995*
❖Production Assistant   *January 1992–October 1992*
❖Researcher   *January 1991–April 1994*

EDUCATION   **Parsons School of Design**   New York, NY
Courses in computer technology.
1995–present

New School for Social Research New York, NY
BA, 1990
Multimedia Studies, Communication

HONORS   **Vista Award, 1994**   Game Design: Story Line
Multimedia Designers Group, Vice President

Pat Jones
77 Boxer Street
New York, New York 10012
212/477/1234
E-mail pjones@jones.surf.com

OBJECTIVE

Music composer position with CD-ROM or
Video Games developer.
   Musician & performer.
   Four years' experience composing and
translating themes and background scores for
video games and for on-line web sites.

Recent clients include:

Wrestlemania V, The Game	Titan Sports, Inc.
Get Back, Bach!	Music Age
Tour of the Grand Canyon	Colorado Strings

COMPUTER SKILLS

Graphics	Word Processing
Communication	Corel Draw
3.0 Ami Pro	Procomm Plus 2.1
Harvard Graphics	WordPerfect
Winfax Pro	Scankit
QuickLink	

Music (Midi Software):

Cakewalk Pro	Band in a Box
Encore Power Tracks Pro	
Finale Midi Scan	

PROFESSIONAL EXPERIENCE

Electronic Music Composer
Daytime Online Music and Sound Library
Brooklyn, New York
March 1992–present
Prepare compositions in the form of midi files for our
commercial clients and for video games.

Radio Host/Producer
"Sunday Classics" NYCN
December 1992–Present
Producer/host of radio music talk show
On-the-job training in audio production and editing.

Music Teacher
St. Michael School
New York, New York
1991–1992
Taught Music to grade 6, 7, and 8 classes as well as
regular grade 6 classes.

Music teacher
Dominican Academy
New York, New York
1990–1991
Taught Music and English as a Second Language to
students in grades 9 to 11.

AWARDS

Senior Scholarship plus several awards of merit for
trombone and vocal performances.
Brooklyn Heights Kiwanis Music Festival
1987–1988 seasons.

Gold Medal in city-wide competition for inventing
musical instruments.
Albany Regional Science Olympics, 1984.

EDUCATION

1990   Bachelor of Education
        Certified to teach music and drama

1989   Bachelor of Music Concentration
        Music Education and Composition

Related Experience

Performer, Trombone
Jazz Knights, 4 piece combo
Sheraton Inn
New York City
1994–present

Panelist
"Cyberspace - Cybermusic"
Forum on Internet Applications for the Arts
January, 1996

Listen to my work on:

http://www.erty.com
http://jazze.nyc.com
http://www.horns.com

PAT JONES

77 Boxer Street   Crystal, Minneapolis 55428   612/ 477-1234

SUMMARY

Trumpet soloist with more than 10 years of performing experience; career includes live and recorded performances.

PROFESSIONAL EXPERIENCE
Trumpet Soloist
1988 to present
Concert Engagements

Symphony Hall, San Francisco "Mahler"
Town Hall, NY POPS
Nevada Philharmonic, Spring Concert Series

Recordings

Julio Iglesias	*"Spanish Heat,"* JK Records
Madonna	*"Baby Love,"* Sire Records
Juilliard Strings	*"Ravel and Others,"* Dix Discs

Contract Musician
1986 to present

MINNEAPOLIS SYMPHONY ORCHESTRA
MINNEAPOLIS, MN

ST. PAUL BALLET ORCHESTRA
ST. PAUL, MN

Instructor /
Trumpet, Flugelhorn, Chamber Music
1980 to present

LAUREN MC GILL MUSIC SCHOOL
ST. PAUL, MN
Provide individualized and group instruction for students of a broad range of ages and abilities. Research instructional materials and methods.

Recruiter
1988 to 1990

HEADLEY MUSIC SCHOOL
ST. PAUL, MN
Conducted formal interviews and auditions with prospective candidates for admission.

PROFESSIONAL TRAINING
◇   Studied at English Conservatory

1988

JUILLIARD SCHOOL OF MUSIC
NEW YORK, NEW YORK

MA, 1987

◇   Studied under Sr. Charles Mangione

1985–1987

MANES SCHOOL OF MUSIC
NEW YORK, NEW YORK

BA, 1984

Pat Jones
77 Boxer Street
Stamford, Connecticut 06750
(203)477-1234
E-mail: pjones@jones.com

OBJECTIVE

Position as manager of new media content; to contribute to the overall development and success of a progressive Internet business organization using my on-line experience,

    ... ability to create and maintain procedures,
    ... to solve problems, and
    ... to communicate effectively to provide solid results.

QUALIFICATIONS

Over 10 years of results-oriented management experience including:
    Strategic and Tactical Operational Management
    Management Analysis
    Project Management
    Cross Functional Facilitation

PROFESSIONAL EXPERIENCE

PIPELINE SERVICES COMPANY   1985–present
Stamford, Connecticut
Manager, Design Operations

Plan and Track over 1500 tasks & issues for the next generation of the Web Service. Lead cross functional teams to resolve issues related to Content, Production and Customer Satisfaction.

Key Accomplishments:
✔ **Manage** and directly responsible for the productivity of 125 Interactive Media Designers.
✔ **Create and manage** project allocation process for the IMD's for an average weekly volume of 55 WEB design projects.
✔ **Strengthened & redefined** 5 traditional Design roles to one by cross training in JAVA. This enables Design Operations to reduce resources per project by over 40%.
✔ **Streamlined** point of contact between other departments improving communications and accountability.

METRO HEALTH   1980–1985
Hartford, Connecticut
Manager, Financial Claims Processing Center

Managed 25 staff members as well as all sub-processes within the claims processing center.

EDUCATION

Fairfield University   1984
Bachelor of Business Administration   **Major:** Marketing
    Minor: Computer Science

Courses in HTML, Web Editing, JAVA, C++

QUALIFICATIONS

Strong knowledge of all aspects of newsroom operations.

Reporting, writing and production skills.

On-air experience interviewing, hosting and reporting.

Working on audio book *"Cooking with the Best"* for Penguin Audio, recipes shared by world-famous cooks
interspersed with interviews and cooking tips; negotiating CD-ROM version. Publication in 1998.

WORK EXPERIENCE

FDEN, New York City

1995–1996

"TODAY'S TABLE" (NEWS MAGAZINE SHOW)

SUBSTITUTE ANCHOR   Fill in as live news show anchor for D.S. Roxie.

FIELD REPORTER   Creatively explore quirky health and/or culinary questions through writing, producing, editing
and reporting in investigative "WHAT'S NEW IN THE KITCHEN" segments.

SEGMENT PRODUCER   Book, write and produce live in studio segments featuring celebrities, health and culinary
experts.

"YOU, ME & WHAT WE EAT" (CULINARY NEWS SHOW)

FIELD PRODUCER   Expanded upon relevant food and health oriented news stories through author and celebrity
bookings, writing, producing and editing of daily stories for live news show.

WWIN NEWSRADIO 100, New York City

1994 to 1995:

PRODUCER/INTERVIEW COORDINATOR   Explored media events by choosing subjects and individuals to be
profiled on afternoon news program. Coordinated airtime, pre-interviewed guests and provided talent with a
detailed fact sheet and lead-in for each interview. Conducted on-air Q & A interviews with affiliate stations
reporting on major stories.

SATELLITE TRUCK OPERATOR   Presided over all technical aspects of production, from locating and establishing
contact with satellite to producing reporter's live updates and feeds.

FREELANCE WRITING

Published in: *NY1 News, George, 20/20, Day & Date, El Dia Nueva York, CableVisiones*

EDUCATION

B.A. Binghamton State University, Binghamton, New York, 1993

Major: English   Minor: Journalism

Graduate Study   Pace University, New York

Courses in public speaking, production and text analysis.

Audio or Video tapes available for your review.

PATJONES
77 Boxer Street   New York, New York 10012
212-477-1234   Cell 212-477-8888 E-mail pjones@jones.com

Pat Jones

77 Boxer Street
New Orleans,
Louisiana
70135

Phone:
504-477-1234
Fax:
504-477-1235

Photography

Video

Multi-Media

Client List and
Portfolio Available

Corporate
and
Individual
Assignments

QUALIFICATIONS

Photographer specializing in industrial, architectural, corporate and special events. Still and video photography. Hypertext presentations. Expert with 35mm film, video formats, and HyperStudio.

PROFESSIONAL EXPERIENCE

Freelance 1990–Present
Established a local reputation as a high-quality, cost-effective alternative to major studios.

Sophisticated corporate multi-media presentations.

Commercial marketing communications projects.

Video memories of special events.

Photo shoots for business and V.I.P. portfolios.

Stills for real estate and architectural purposes.

HIGGENS STUDIO 1985–1989
Norwalk, CT
Photographer for weddings, private and corporate events

QUAD IMAGING LABS 1983–1985
Chicago, IL
Processed film and videos for this high volume lab

EDUCATION

CHICAGO SCHOOL OF PHOTOGRAPHY
Comprehensive Photography Certificate, 1985

LA SALLE UNIVERSITY
Bachelor of Arts Degree, 1982

Additional training in multi-media at Hyper Studios

"Stunning photos ... captured the event with grace and clarity." CEO, Sun Oil Co.
"Presentations for our marketing group were A-1!" Execusales, Inc. President
"Our wedding was the most important day in our lives, and Pat took the day and made a video full of memories for a lifetime." Mr. and Mrs. James Grisholm

Pat Jones

77 Boxer Street
New York, New York 10012
212-477-1234
FAX 212-477-1235

OBJECTIVE

To work for innovative, active photographer; able to relocate.
Wide range of talents to offer, from office manager to prop preparation to purchasing agent.
Over 22 years' experience.
Flexible, easy to work with; personable; proven ability to meet deadlines and budgets.
Excellent organizational skills, PC literate.

"Snapshot" EXPERIENCE

Worked as a stylist for twenty-two years. Tasks have ranged from locating an extremely rare antique and negotiating its rental to sewing costumes and building room-size sets for use as photo props. Functioned as office manager and purchasing agent in addition to stylist and would be willing to handle these responsibilities again.

WORK CHRONOLOGY

1974 to 1995   **Chief stylist & office manager**   Tribeca Arts/ Alex Greene
Photographer specializing in interior and product shots. Clients included NY Times, Home and Garden, El Diario, Architectural Digest, Bradlee's Department Store, Footlocker.

Supervised secretary, bookkeeper, and receptionist, while assuming major responsibility for all styling. When necessary, I hired additional persons to help with set and prop preparation and supervised their work.

1973–1974   **Window dresser**   Macy's Department Store
Responsible for in-store and 34th Street windows.

1971–1973   **Office support**   Jacob Reiss, fashion photographer
Booked and helped select models, bought photography supplies, and kept books for business in addition to secretarial responsibilities.

EDUCATION

Georgia State University   B.A., Fine Arts, 1971.

SKILLS

Fluent in French.
Computer skills: MS Office, Microsoft Works

INTERESTS

Travel, art, reading.

Pat Jones PhotoJournalist
77 Boxer Street Grand Rapids, MI 49503
616-477-1234 Fax 616-477-1235

Photography portfolio available

Objective Photo-journalist with four years of international freelance experience and sales to major news services seeking further affiliations in the capacity of an independent contractor or staff position.

Photograph

Photo Caption

· Owner and expert user of Haselblad and Nikon cameras with a full complement of supporting equipment.

· Established relationships with principal commercial photo processing centers in New York and Europe.

· Fluent in European and Asian languages; raised overseas as a diplomatic dependent.

· Press credentials certified in major markets.

· Skilled in darkroom and film developing.

Professional Assignments
1992–Present
Freelance photo journalist

1995 – Eastern European coverage of liberation movements.
Time Magazine
1994 – Colombian drug war and other Central American issues.
The New York Times
1993 – Peoples Republic of China—update on student activism.
The London Times
1993 – Photo feature contract on Japanese economy.
The Daily Herald

1988–1991
Staff Photographer
The Washington Post

Congress from the human perspective.

Election coverage as a traveling journalist alternating parties.

Crime in the nation's capital.

Education

Bachelor of Science
Journalism
Davidson College, MN   1988

Photograph

Photo Caption

Pat Jones, P.I.

77 Boxer Street Trumbull, Connecticut 06611
203-477-1234 FAX 203-477-1235
CELL 203-677-1234

Overview

Seasoned law enforcement and security officer with police and licensed private investigator experience seeks affiliation with an established investigative firm in the tri-state area.

Capabilities

INSTITUTIONAL

Urban police officer in the capacities of patrolman and detective.
Knowledge of enforcement and judicial bureaucracies.
Acquainted with and respected by principals and functionaries throughout the regional law enforcement establishment.
Working knowledge of civil and criminal statutes.

RESEARCH

Government agency files.
Telephone investigation.
Personal interviewing.

SURVEILLANCE

Domestic evidence gathering.
Video and photographic techniques.
Pursuit and documentation of movements.

Experience

1987–Present	Security Consultant, Self-employed.
1981–1987	Detective, Stamford, CT Municipal Police Department
1978–1987	Patrolman, NY Police Department, Queens, NY

Education

Associate in Applied Science
Criminology
Borough of Manhattan Community College   New York, NY, 1978

Licenses

New York, New Jersey, Connecticut, Rhode Island Private Investigation
Licenses in good standing

Honors

Police Benevolent Society Guest Speaker, Spring Dinner
"Investigation Techniques in Cyberspace"   1996
Community Leadership Award, YMCA   1995
Sharpshooter, Grade 1   1980
(Qualified annually, through 1996)
Technology Liaison, FBI   1985–1987

PAT JONES
77 BOXER STREET
NEW YORK, NEW YORK 10012
PHONE: 212-477-1234 FAX: 212-477-1235

—SUMMARY—

Expert designer experienced in film and theater.
Tony-nominee for production of Disney's
"Pinocchio."
Detail-oriented professional who has spent
entire professional life in film and theater.
"Worked my way up" from carpenter to set building
to set design to planning entire production value.

—PROFESSIONAL HIGHLIGHTS—

Production Designer for:
"Evita: She Did It Her Way"
Director M. Ciccione

"Heroes of the Fall"
Director Wayne Boggs

"100 Years of Broadway"
Broadhurst Theater
Director Jean Janos

"Les Mis on Ice"
Disney IceCapades
Director Matthew Barnes

Jean Cocteau Repertory Company
Playwrights' Marathon

—CURRENT EMPLOYMENT—

Disney Productions, New York
Since 1995
Production Designer, Tombstone Films Division
Production values for series of
short films for TV
on America's Western History;
to be released in 1997.

—EMPLOYMENT HISTORY—

Tribeca FilmWorks, New York
1990–1994
Production Design

Astoria Studios, New York
1983–1989
Production Manager, 1988–1989
Set Design, 1986–1988
Set Building, Furnishings, 1983–1985

Star Productions
1980–1983
Carpenter, Electrician

—TRAINING—

Manhattan College
Masters Program in progress
Estimated graduation date, June 1997

Brooklyn College
BA, Literature 1987

New School for Social Research, New York
Courses in theater arts, history of the theater,
film history, set design
1979–1984

ICT (Industrial Career Training)
Hoboken, NJ
1978

—PROFESSIONAL AFFILIATIONS—

Broadway Guild
DIFFA Board
Association of Production Designers, Treasurer
Lecturer: New School for Social Research

Pat Jones
77 Boxer Street
New York, New York 10012
Phone: 212-477-1234
Fax: 212-477-1235

OBJECTIVE   **Public Affairs Director**
- Veteran news reporter and talk show host
- Initiated programs for local communities on-air
- Production experience

EMPLOYMENT

1983–Present
Public Affairs Director
Host of "Eye on New Jersey"; reporter
WNJ - TV, Secaucus, NJ

Public Affairs Director responsible for moderating panel discussions and special programs on topical issues, as well as talk show responsibilities. Recent topics included:

"Negative Campaigns: Do They Work?"
"How Much Should the Federal Government Control TV Viewing?"
"The "Newest" Diet Pill"
"Fake Fat? or Just a Fake?"

- Established Community Bulletin Boards, free announcements of community events for local groups and non-profit organizations.
- *"Community Group of the Month"* highlighted on Sunday Evening News.
- Established intern program with inner-city high schools.

Host live talk show *"Eye on New Jersey"* presented daily as a public relations and community project.

- Given full responsibility for the hour show; ratings up 1.8 points since initiating spontaneous interviews and upgrading guest list.
- Designed set, created opening and close, procured clothing sponsor to furnish daily wardrobe, lined up and scheduled all guests.
- Guests are briefed minimally, but prefer spontaneity of the largely unrehearsed interview. Guests have included: U.S. senators, visiting actors and celebrities, as well as concerned citizens within the station's viewing area.

Member of investigative news team. Developed and followed leads; wrote and edited features and news stories. Organized team for location shoots, arranged interviews. News stories reported:

"Crime in Our Midst" on political graft in local government
"Tough Learning" on difficulties at NJ State Board of Education
"Recycling: Is it Worth It?" on the environment

Page 1 of 2

1980–1983
WRTS-TV, Princeton, NJ
Traffic and Continuity Director
Responsible for daily log as well as continuity; wrote commercial copy and station promotional material. In addition, did occasional on-air spots and voice-overs; filled in for "Princeton Profiles" host.

1978–1980
WEVF-TV, Houston, TX
Production Assistant
Designed sets and graphics; served as liaison between the technical and instructional personnel at educational television station.

1975–1978
WKYW-TV, Columbus, OH
Continuity and production
Kept production logs; supported and interfaced with all areas of production.

EDUCATION

Baruch College   1978
BA, Journalism

AFFILIATIONS

National Press Club
New Jersey Broadcasters Association
Princeton Chamber of Commerce
District 7, School Board Member
NJPB Citizens Advisory Board

Videotapes of on-air programs available.

Pat Jones

Public Relations • Marketing

77 Boxer Street
New York, New York 10012
212-477-1234

OBJECTIVE

Management position in public relations or marketing with a forward-thinking, aggressive company that needs a professional with excellent writing, organization and promotion skills.

Special expertise in health care and sports industries.
Computer literate.

PROFESSIONAL ACCOMPLISHMENTS

Public Relations, Marketing and Event Planning
Coordinated public relations and marketing efforts including writing and placement of press releases and media advisories, securing interviews, developing story ideas and designing media kits.
Wrote, produced and recorded radio public service announcements.

Developed marketing strategy for instructional video, with target markets and audience demographics.

Coordinated and hosted regional and national training workshops and agency events.
Planned and oversaw department and agency fundraising events.
Researched and collaborated on grant proposals.
Compiled national mailing lists for marketing strategy.

Editorial and Creative Services
Created and edited program brochures, newsletters and agency catalogs.
Edited and proofread publications for professional sports leagues.
Designed cover for instructional video as well as advertisements for national and international publications.

Created and designed program displays for agency events and corporate outreach.

Administration
Hired, managed, supervised and trained staff of 15.
Prepared annual department budget of $3.8M and bi-weekly payroll.
Developed and implemented department policy, including preparation of member policy manual, staff manuals and instructor training program.
Tracked and analyzed quarterly statistics.
Participated in staff team-building and diversity training.

Program Planning and Development
Conducted needs assessments and program evaluations.
Developed, implemented and conducted testing, orientation and evaluation.
Designed and implemented corporate exercise programs for several large companies.
Developed, scheduled and instructed adult and youth fitness programs.

PROFESSIONAL EXPERIENCE

1993–1996 **Director, Public Relations and Marketing Consultant**
Egret Sports Enterprises, Inc., Eastchester, NY

1992–1993 **Coordinator, Health and Fitness Department**
YWCA of Indianapolis, Indianapolis, IN

1990–1992 **Coordinator, Fitness Program**
Hartford Region YWCA, Hartford, CT

1988–1990 **Office Manager**
Road Runners Sports Medical Center, Hartford, CT (1988)

COMPUTER SKILLS

Proficiency on Macintosh and IBM compatibles.
Competency with Word Perfect 5.1; Microsoft Word 6.0; Works 3.0;
Excel; Publisher; Windows 3.1; PageMaker 5.0.

Proficient on America On-line, Prodigy, Microsoft Network

Experience with Access.

EDUCATION

Master of Education, Health Fitness
Antioch College, Yellow Springs, OH

Bachelor of Science, Sports Medicine
Kent State University, Kent, OH

AFFILIATIONS AND CERTIFICATIONS

New York Marketers Group
Road Skaters of America
Certified Aerobics Instructor-National Fitness Association
Asics and Reebok Instructor Alliances

COMMUNITY INVOLVEMENT

Kent State University, New York Metro Alumni Assoc.
Chairperson, Events Committee

New York City Marathon
Communications Committee

Sloan Kettering Cancer Care Center
Conference Planning Committee

Literacy Volunteers of America
English as a Second Language Tutor

PAT JONES
77 BOXER STREET
GREENWICH, CT 06830
(203)477-1234   FAX (203)477-1235

SUMMARY
Award winning journalist with more than 15 years of experience in television, public relations and marketing. Proven expertise in launching creative and corporate campaigns from inception to completion.

MAJOR ACCOMPLISHMENTS

Public Relations

Media spokesperson for New York City politician.
Manager of a 6 person staff responsible for all promotional and advertising projects.
Provided leadership in generation of press releases, statements and speeches.
Consistently landed client exposure on all major media.

Marketing/Advertising

As head of advertising and promotion for boutique-sized firm added major hotel and conference center to client roster.
Video producer/copywriter creating commercials from start to finish for major global clients in fashion and beverage industries. Came up with original concepts, wrote scripts and devised story board. Booked camera crews and scouted locations.
Directed shoots and completed final cuts with editors.

TV/Communications

News reporter for television stations in New York City and Cincinnati. Conducted on-camera interviews and off-camera screening. Supervised location shoots. Wrote segments and recorded voice-overs.

Entrepreneurial Sales

Started own business.
Business to business marketing of personalized items.
Media trained corporate clients for pitching controversial issues and fielding questions from the press.
Special promoted features for newscasts won high ratings and over $1M in revenue for stations airing them.

PAGE 1 OF 2

WORK HISTORY

1994 to Present	*High Value Ventures,* Hartford, CT President
1991–1993	*High Impact Communications,* Stamford, CT Writer/Media Trainer
1988–1990	*Corporate Communications,* Reno, NV Copywriter Video Producer
1987–1988	*Office of the President* *of the New York City Council* Press Secretary
1982–1987	*WCBS-TV* Reporter/Producer for *"Eyewitness News"*

EDUCATION

1980	B.S., Babson College Major: Communications

PROFESSIONAL AWARDS

Associated Press for Spot News

Pat Jones

77 Boxer Street
Bonita Beach, Florida 33960
813-477-1234 Fax 813-477-1235
E-mail pjones@jones.com

Summary: **Experienced recreation director for adult, teen and children's activities.**

✿ Established a *Kids' Fun Club* for childcare at resort; up to 25 children paid enrollment daily.

✿ Augmented beach activities with Nature Walks hosted by local experts.

✿ Extended lunchtime fashion shows with a *"Back to School"* show for teens as well as a *"Surfing Dudes"* show; both events have had "standing room only" for the last 2 seasons.

✿ Activities initiated in past 4 years have increased profits in recreation center 33%.

Experience: *Sundial Beach Resort*   Bonita Springs, FL
Recreation Director   1991–Present
Hire and supervise staff of 15 recreation counselors for adult, teen and children's programs starting at 8AM through 10PM seven days each week. Book additional entertainment and specialists for special events.
Write monthly newsletter for events and promotions distributed to 350 hotel guests.
Schedule Regional Tennis Camp June–August, Golf Camp November–January.
Responsible for annual budget of $120,000.

Recreation Counselor   1988–1991
Supervised programs for children and adults.
Assisted director in scheduling programs and staff hours.
Hosted *"Teen Night Out"* Dance and Pool Party weekly.

Beach Assistant   1986–1987
Assisted hotel guests with beach chairs, towels, umbrellas.

Education: Manatee Community College
Punta Gorda, FL
AS Liberal Arts, 1988

Microsoft Skills Center, Fort Lauderdale, 1988
MS Word, Excel, Access, Internet Explorer

**Related
Training
and Skills:** Red Cross Lifesaving and CPR Course, 1988
Registered Lifeguard, Florida State, qualified annually
Competitive Doubles Player, Sharks Team Florida
Accomplished Surfer, Volleyball Player, Swimmer, Sailor

Pat Jones
77 Boxer Street
Queens Village, New York 11429
212-477-1234

Objective

Restaurant Manager with a growing national chain. Willing to relocate.

✗ 8 years' experience in all phases of restaurant management.

✗ Within two years vaulted restaurant to top 10 of 550 in overall profitability.

Professional Experience

MAMA ANNA'S	Bridgeport, CT
General Manager	**1988 to present**

Manage all operations of this highly successful, 300 seat Italian restaurant with annual sales exceeding $3.5M. Open 7 days a week and holidays.

Oversee personnel, finance, food preparation, purchasing, marketing, customer service, maintenance, and security.

Coordinated all details of restaurant opening.

Received *Store of the Month Award* during sixth month of operation.

Selected by top management to participate in national management meetings.

✗ Budgeting Seminar, 1995

✗ Personnel Practices, 1994

✗ Marketing Workshop, 1993

✗ Health and Safety Issues, 1991

CUCINA MIA	Trumbull, CT
Assistant Manager	**1985 to 1988**
Host/Waiter	**1983 to 1985**

150 seat informal family-style restaurant; banquet facilities.

Education

CONNECTICUT COLLEGE	Waterbury, CT
A.S. in **Business Administration**	1983

Pat Jones
WRITER - PRODUCER

SUMMARY

Multi-talented television and movie professional screenwriter and producer; developed original movies and TV series; flexible, organized, proven ability to adhere to budgets and shooting schedules. Over twenty-four years of experience.

Writer of highly-rated television movies and sit-coms:

"Toad-boy"	ABC
"Middle-Aged Ninja Mom"	Time-Warner
"EEEK ... the cat!"	New Line Cinema
"Cousin It"	Fox 5

Screenwriter and producer for acclaimed TV series:

"Reconstruction"	Ken Burns
"Under NYC Streets"	Guiliani Productions/CNN
"Hudson River: The Future"	Robert Redford/Sundance

PROFESSIONAL ACCOMPLISHMENTS

Executive Producer
"Doomed Lake" for Nickelodeon.
This 90-minute pilot will serve as Nickelodeon's first movie-style adventure series.

Screenwriter
"Robert in Love," an original screenplay to be completed in early 1997.

Co-Screenwriter/ Executive Producer
"Clueless Dad" for Viacom Television.
A feature-length comedy based on the movie.
Released on Showtime in 1996.

Executive Producer
"Innocent and Unarmed." This CBS movie of the week starred Kate Jackson and Gerald McRaney.

Co-Screenwriter
"Moon Over Columbus," under option to Todd /AO-TAE.
Feature-length romantic comedy about a mother, a daughter, and a rock star.

Co-Executive Producer
"Old Affairs," distributed by Arrow Entertainment.
Comedy was the first film selected for screening by the Kodak "First Look" Film Festival.

Continued ...

77 Boxer Street   New York, New York 10012   212.477.1234

PROFESSIONAL WORK HISTORY

1987–90:   **Executive Vice President**   Stardust Pictures, New York.
Executive Producer, *"The Spencerville Stories"*
Three one-hour television movies produced for USA Playhouse.

1983–87:   **Director of Development & Production**   J-B Productions, New York.
Associate Producer, *"Trackdown: In Search of a Serial Killer,"* a CBS movie of the week starring Michael J. Fox.
Associate Producer, *"Out of The Tunnels,"* a CBS movie of the week starring Sharon Stone and Michael Douglas.
Associate Producer, *"Day Freeze,"* a CBS late night series.

1981–83:   **Director of Development**   Universal Entertainment, New York.
Associate Producer, *"The Red and the Black,"* a mini-series for ABC television.
Co-Producer, *"Kreskin,"* a special for Ted Brown Television Syndication.

1979–81:   **Director of Development**   A. Silver, New York.
Associate Producer, *"Autumn Kills,"* a feature film released by MGM.

1975–78:   **Director of Development and Acquisition**   Cine-Nation, New York.
Theatrical acquisitions for distribution including *"Johnny and His Gun," "Oh, Momma," "Doophus,"* and *"Mahler in Love."*
Associate Producer, *"All the Kind Friends,"* an ABC television movie, starring Stacy Keach and Robby Benson.

1972–74:   **Theatrical Agent**   National Agency, New York.

EDUCATION

New York University, Tisch School of the Arts
Film and Television Production   MA, 1975

Columbia University   BA, 1972

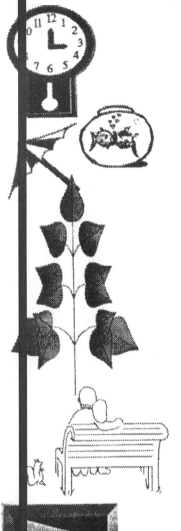

☥ᴀᴛ JONES
77 BOXER STREET
NEW YORK, NEW YORK 10012
212-477-1234
BEEPER 212-477-9999

OBJECTIVE
Position with theatrical or movie company; freelance.
 Experience in film, video, television, theater.
 Historical or period pieces a specialty; expert research.
 Reliable and expert contacts with prop houses.

PROFESSIONAL EXPERIENCE
FEATURE FILMS
"Once In Awhile"	Sundance Features, Robert Redford
"No … No"	Nanette Films, Martin Scorsese
"1980"	Bo-Ring Films, Michael J. Fox
"Ting-a-ling"	Disney, Dennis Hopper

TELEVISION MOVIES
"It Happened Here"	Motown, Deneice Williams
"Olympic Fever"	Up-n-Down Cinema, K. Wallack
"Bronx Bomber"	Yankee Productions, Bebe Ruth

THEATER
"On the Road"	Vivian Beaumont, John Travolta
"New York?"	Cocteau Theater, Mary Monti
"#1"	Theater of Absurd, R. Julianie

VIDEO
"Tonight"	Smashing Pumpkins
"MTV Beach House"	Summer, 1996

COMMERCIALS
BMW	GTE
NCR	WPLJ-Radio
NYNEX	Yves Rocher

AFFILIATIONS
 Member I.A. Local 52

EDUCATION
New School for Social Research Furnishings	1990
Mercy College BA, English Literature	1988

QUALIFICATIONS: Art professional with 14 successful years of broad-based experience encompassing all phases of creative set designs, backdrops, miniature sets, props and centerpieces.

- **Creative, innovative and ingenious** detailing themes and styles.
- **Excellent technical skills** with the ability to conceptualize, visualize and create original artwork from sketch and layout to final production.
- **Able to master new concepts,** ideas and practices.
- **Proficient in problem identification, evaluation and resolution.** Skilled at prioritizing workloads and handling multiple projects simultaneously and efficiently with emphasis on meeting production requirements and deadlines.
- **Strong illustration** and presentation skills.

EXPERIENCE:

DAZZLING EVENTS
Oceanside, NY
1990–Present
ART DIRECTOR

- **Develop projects** from initial concept, first sample to presentation.
- **Supervise the daily activities** of the Art department.
- **Determine desired image** based on emerging trends, styles and client preferences.
- **Create original sketches** and designs for private and corporate functions.
- **Work closely with associate** artists and art coordinators in all phases of production from materials sourcing and purchasing to final production of set designs and backdrops.
- **Review client and specs** when creating desired themes to impact optimally on occasion.
- **Research various sources** of props and negotiate cost within budget allocation.
- **Select desired accessories** to complement designs; formulate themes to achieve design and production portrayal.
- **Direct photographers** and clients to achieve a diversity of moods within layout requirements.
- **Communicate** desired space, background, lighting and "design look."
- **Utilize established system** of moods for innovative ideas and desired effect.

❖

CONFIDENT STUDIOS
Forest Hills, NY
1987–1990
PHOTOGRAPHER/
ASSOCIATE ARTIST

- **Organized** all aspects of "on-location" photo shoots and oversaw staff activities.
- **Explored and evaluated** locations for photography; handled the completion of all documentation necessary to shoot on various premises.
- **Participated** in meetings to evaluate photography and photo direction; acted on suggestion and feedback, and arrived at an acceptable plan of action.

❖

NEW YORK TELEPHONE
Brooklyn, NY
1982–1987
PRODUCT DEVELOPMENT
TEAM

- **Involved** in all special projects: designed logos and packaging labels for products.
- **Handled** all visual merchandising and display.

MARK WHITE AGENCY
New York, NY
1979–1982
GRAPHICS DESIGN INTERN

- **Prepared** pre-production & finished artwork.

❖

EDUCATION:

ARTS STUDENTS LEAGUE
New York, NY
1992–1994
Computer Graphics, Theater Production, Set Design

CENTER FOR MEDIA ARTS
New York, NY
1991–1992
CAD, Computer Animation, Paste-Up Mechanicals and Photography

Pat Jones
77 Boxer Street
New York, NY
10012

212-477-1234
Fax 212-477-1235
❖
Portfolio available
❖

Pat Jones
77 Boxer Street
Lowers, CA 90210
213-477-1234   Fax 213-477-1235
E-mail pjones@jones.surf.com

Photo

Summary: **National and regional champion surfer; live event and television sports commentator.**
Winner of *King of the Reef Competition*, 1992;
US Open 1989 & 1991; *Australian Open*, 1986
Second-Place Winner of *NSSA*, 1990
Broadcasting Experience: Lead commentator US Sports Network *Billabong Pro-Am*, February, 1996; *Umbro Championships*, December, 1995; ESPN-2 commentator on *Honolulu Surf-Off*, October, 1995

Highlights: Internationally recognized world-class surfer
Experienced surfing and doing "color" in locations in Philippines, Japan, US, Mexico, Costa Rica, Bahamas, Australia, New Zealand; wealth of anecdotes and surfing history add value. Personal knowledge of current and up-and-coming surfers; excellent interview rapport with surfers and audience.
Designed "jones board" for BJ Boards, Inc.
Cover of "Sports Illustrated," April, 1990: *Surfer of the Year*

Experience: **Owner/Manager**
1992–present
Surf Safari Shop   Lowers, CA
Order all merchandise; assist customers in choosing boards; organize promotions and advertising. Sponsor local surfing contests.
Hire and supervise staff of 3.
Provide surfing lessons.

Consultant
1986–1993
"No Fear" Sportswear   Venice, CA
Provided insight and recommendations for surf and beach wear; modeled clothing for print ads. Made personal appearances to promote clothing line in US and Mexico.

Education: Pacifica High School   Venice Beach, CA
General Degree, 1984
Bookkeeping courses, Lowers Community College, 1993

Affiliations: National Member Surf Board
Association of Sports Broadcasters

Video and audio tapes available for your review.

Pat Jones
77 Boxer Street
Bronx, New York 10471
718-477-1234

Summary:
Involved on numerous video, theater, TV and film productions over past 10 years.
Perfect safety record; insured and bonded.
Expert in martial arts, stage fighting, car/train chases, pyro and fire stunts.
Member SAG, AFTRA

Professional Experience:
Highlights:

Stunt Coordinator
ViaCom Film, *"Predator 4"*   Director: Ron Howard
Multimedia Productions, *"Ozzie & Harriet Revisited"*   Director: Ida Lupino
Vista Visions Videos, *"Porno for Pyros"*   Director: "MAD" De Luca

Assistant Stunt Coordinator
ABC-TV, *"All Your Children"*   1993–1994
Howard Beach Promotions, *"Sunset to Dawn"*   Director: Nancy Devine
Music World, *"Rap Around the World"*   Director: Iggy Pop

Stunts
Warner Brothers, *"Rodeo Life"*   Director: James H. Orse
Chun King Films, *"Yakuze Warrior"*   Director: Charles E. Chan
NBC-TV, *"When the World Goes Round"*   1990–1992
WWF, *"Wrestlemania Goes Wild"*   1990
SonyPlaystation Video, *"Martial Arts Kick-Off"*   1996

Special Skills:
3rd Degree Black Belt, Aikido
2nd Degree Black Belt, Goju Karate
Horseback riding, stunt and show riding; dressage
Swimming, diving
Archery, sharpshooting (gun and rifle)
Stage fighting (knives, swords, lances, maces); fencing
Tai Chi Chuan
Dancing, gymnastics

Training:

Grandmaster Gai Djo Doung   1996–present
Tai Chi Chuan Association   1994–present
The Bond Street Dojo   1992–1995
USA Oyama's Karate   1987–1992
Instructor:
Asphalt Green   1992–present
Swimming, diving, fencing

TELEVISION DIRECTOR (FREELANCE, BROCHURE FORMAT)

QUALIFICATIONS

Over twenty-five years' experience directing movies, specials, series, commercials and corporate films for TV, cable TV and independent clients.

EXPERIENCE

Jones Production Company
New York, New York
Owner 1990–present

"It Is a Matter of Choice"
National Organization of Women, 1996
"Questions of Loyalty"
Turner Broadcasting, 1996

"An Attack of Yankee Fever: 1996"
NY Yankee Organization, 1996
"How NOT to Run an Election"
NYC News Special, 1995

"Where Are Our Kids?"
YMCA-YWCA, 1995

"Music—It is in Our Blood"
The Osmond Family, 1994

Commercials:
Alka-Seltzer
Stride-Rite Shoes
Nike
NYC Marathon '95
D.A.R.E.
Yahoo!

Corporate Films:
AT & T Universal Credit
Metropolitan Transit Authority Training
GTE
Electric Library
Chase Manhattan Bank
NY State Department of Taxation and
Finance
O.T.B.
McGraw-Hill Business Publications

ACCOMPLISHMENTS

1996 Advertising Age Directors' Award
"Alka-Seltzer Come-back"

1994 Museum of Broadcasting
Moderator
"What Is RIGHT with TV?"

1991 Golden Plum Award
TV Directors Guild

Three made-for-TV movies
nominated for Emmy awards.

Collaborator on acclaimed series:
"New York — Past & Present"
New York Historical Society

EDUCATION

1988 Tribeca Film School

1986 Fordham University, New York
BA

Experienced TV director, writer and editor for broadcast, cable and corporate video production

• • • • • • • •

Computer graphics
3D rendering and animation
Photojournalism and photography
Marketing and promotion

• • • • • • • •

PAT JONES
77 Boxer Street
New York, New York 10012
212-477-1234   Fax 212-477-1235
Beeper 212-678-1234

Videos available for your review:
Commercials
TV
Corporate

Pat Jones

77 Boxer St.,
Richmond Hill, NY 11496

Home phone: (718) 477-1234
Pager number: (712) 477-1234

Objective:	To secure a position with a post-production or television facility

Experience: **Madison Square Garden,** New York City. 1992 to Present.
Assistant Editor/Off-Line Editor (Sports Desk) performing dubbing and Quality Control activities; also edited promotional pieces together for library and affiliates; loaded various tape, including Sony D2, machines for on-line editor. Other activities include recording and playback of sporting events aired on MSG network; served as Tape Operator responsible for routing and setting up the Beta and one inch machines.

Big Apple TV Services Inc. 1989–1991
Clients Included: FoxFive and Phil Donahue
On-line Editor (Master Control), Tape Operator and Assistant Editor.
Activities included playback of news segments and recording shows produced. Also edited news packages, B-roll, and sound on taped segments.

Skills:

Avid Off Line Editing System	GrassValley Switcher 200-1
Grass Valley VPE 141 Editor	Ampex ADO
Dubner 20k	Quanta Font
Grass Valley 100	Ross-Russ 201A
Sony BVU 900-950	Betacam BCB65
Sony BVH3100	Sony PVW 2800-2600
Yamaha Audio Board	BTS Digital Video File Server
Sony D2	

Training: Several Courses at DCTV, continuing at present

Reel available on request

Pat Jones
77 Boxer Street
Manasquan, NJ 08736
908-477-1234   908-477-1235 Fax

OBJECTIVE: A production position in television or videography.

SUMMARY OF QUALIFICATIONS

Demonstrated expertise and talents in all phases and areas of studio and field production. Proven problem solver, calm under pressure, high ethics and character. Computer literate.

Gained first-hand exposure to all aspects of television production including research, post-production, floor management, and technical direction. Knowledge and expertise in the areas of

TIME CODE EDITING	VIDEO SWITCHERS
CHYRON	RESEARCH/WRITING
CAMERA TECHNIQUES	LIVE TELEVISION
LIGHTING	STUDIO OPERATION
FIELD PRODUCTION	EMERGING TECHNOLOGIES
FILM COMPOSITION	SOUND

ACCOMPLISHMENTS

Video Production - Hands-on video production including time-code editing. Used studio to produce a project that involved directing, lighting, sound, switching and supervising the crew.

Editing - Hi-8, VHS and 3/4 inch Beta machines, both on-line and off-line editing. Familiar with non-linear editing. Edited commercials into programs.

Audio Mixing - Recorded audio both in the studio and in the field and have mixed television programs, including news, sports, personalities and multi-lingual.

Wrote news stories, advertisements, public service announcements and documentary scripts in an academic setting for on-the-job preparation.

Received television credits for over 50 individual television episodes. Covered local political events with a mobile production unit.

Production Operations - Helped set up television sets including cameras, scenery, microphones and lights. Monitored audio levels in television programs including lead-in music. Operated a studio and field production camera. Served as studio floor director. Taped sporting events; helped set up equipment.

PROFESSIONAL EXPERIENCE

Independent Contractor   1995–Present
    Provide a range of media production functions including set design, lighting and conception for commercial and non-profit clients.

Partial Client List:

NJ BELL/CORPORATE	NEWPORT MALL/BBDO
TRAMPS	INDIGO GIRLS VIDEO
WESTBETH THEATER	ELECTRIC LIBRARY

CONTINUED ON THE NEXT PAGE

Video Amore Jersey City, NJ   1995–1996
Clerk
> Assisted customers with renting videotapes. Updated computer system. Maintained video library. Performed cash control. Trained and supervised new employees. Collected overdue rental charges.

TalkTV @54 Secaucus, NJ   1993–1995
Production Assistant
> Assisted in all aspects of production for local origination television show, both live and pre-recorded. Gained skills with TV cameras, computer graphics, audio mixing and linear editing. Responded to customer inquiries for advertisement. Used switchers and gained first-hand experience on editing systems.

EDUCATION

B.A. Degree in Mass Communication, Concentration in Television Production
BOSTON COLLEGE, Boston   1995

B.A. Degree in Political Science, Concentration in Research Methods, Minor in Sociology
BOSTON COLLEGE   1993

SKILLS

PC training: WordPerfect, LOTUS 1-2-3
AVID editing

AFFILIATIONS

Member of the National Broadcasting Society, 1995
Alumni Board, BOSTON COLLEGE

Pat Jones
77 Boxer Street
Santa Marina, California 93455
805.477.1234
805.477.1235 fax
805.477.9999 beeper

QUALIFICATIONS   Strong pre-production and production experience.
Diversified public relations experience.
Exceptional organizational skills.

EXPERIENCE

Beach Television, Los Angeles, CA   1994–1996
Production Coordinator *"You Be the Judge"* Torn Pants Productions
Liaison between Buena Vista Television and post production. Supervised the duties of all Production Assistants, Production Secretary and Receptionist (staff totaled 35).
Coordinated trafficking of show material to Buena Vista executives. Responsible for shipping daily shows to satellite for air across the nation.

The Sunshine Group, Malibu, CA   1993–1994
Production Coordinator *"Talk Time"* Fox Television
Liaison between production and below the line.
Responsible for putting together budgets up to $750,000; handling all crew invoicing and payroll requests.
Coordinated trafficking of show set and set elements.
Booked stage locations for show.
Scheduled crews and production services; including, but not limited to, lighting, camera, catering, lighted backdrops.

Quantas Productions, San Diego, CA   1992–1993
Production Coordinator
Public relations liaison between clients and talent.
Coordinated and supervised all visiting foreign production teams.
Handled hotel bookings and locations scouting for production on the West Coast. Executed permits and fee arrangements for all locations.
Coordinated client, crew and talent transportation.
Coordinated the trafficking of all production elements.

RELATED EXPERIENCE

Boom Operator for the feature *"Blue Punk Life,"* a Mauve World Production, Distributed by Orion Pictures, 1992

EDUCATION

College of the West, San Diego, CA 1991
Major: Psychology
Minor: Political Science

PAT JONES

77 Boxer Street • Dona Ana, NM 88032 • 505. 477.1234 • FAX 505. 477. 1235

OBJECTIVE: **Position in drama department of major university or professional theater group.**

EDUCATION:

BACHELOR OF ARTS IN DRAMA
New Mexico State University
Las Cruces, NM 1991

THEATRICAL EXPERIENCE:

DIRECTORIAL EXPERIENCE
- **N.M.S.U. Drama Department**
"Don't Pick the Daisies" (1990) - Director
"Twelfth Night" (1989) - Assistant Director
"The Line" (1988) - Assistant Director

- **Youth Theatre**
"Cinderella" (1986) - Assistant Director

STAGE MANAGEMENT EXPERIENCE
- **N.M.S.U. Drama Department**
"Uninvited" (1986) - Stage Manager

TECHNICAL EXPERIENCE
- **N.M.S.U. Drama Department**
"Ten Little Indians" (1988) - Master Electrician
Shakespeare Festival (1988) - Sound Engineer
"Brigadoon" (1987) - Shift Crew Chief

·Drama Festival (1987) - Construction and Lights

- **Spectrum Players**
"Once Upon a Mattress" (1986) - Spot Operator
"Hair" (1986) - Flys
"South Pacific" (1986) - Spot Operator

EMPLOYMENT HISTORY:

New Mexico State University
Drama Department (1986–1996)

Pat Jones

77 Boxer Street
Irvine, CA 92720
(714) 477-1234   Beeper (714) 477-9999

^^

Qualifications

Unique ability to design to concept/story.
Multi-media experience.
Design Experience:
interior ... landscape ... furniture ... lighting ... sound ... signage ... wardrobe ... electrical.
Designed for art departments of film, theater and TV productions.

Areas of Special Competence

- Project Planning & Budgets
- Cost Control & Containment
- Advertising & Publicity
- Purchasing & Bartering

- Customer & Public Relations
- Historical Accuracy Research
- Quality Assurance & Quality Control
- Meeting Time Constraints

Established and monitored accounts with property and rental houses, hired construction and running crews, and managed budget and payroll. Productions included:

- **Film** ... *"Teen Age Mystery Game," "Waterworld 2," "Waterloo"*
- **TV** ... *"Under the Trees," "Suburban Love," "In My Heart"*
- **Theater** ... *"Antigone," "Babe," "Pushing the Envelope"*
- **Trade Shows & Expos** ... *LA Auto Show, Washington State Agricultural Expo, CyberTeck Trade Show*

Weekly script breakdowns reviewed to determine set adjustments for daytime television soap operas production site with 250 employees on show. Determined weekly studio ground plans, prepared weekly scenic breakdown packets, designed sets, and maintained art department set records.

Drafted set plans and details, furniture design, property design, construction for theatrical production.

Employment Chronology

SCENIC DESIGNER / PRODUCTION DESIGNER	Freelance	1994–Present
SCENIC DESIGNER	Fox5-TV *"Jenny Springer Show"*	1995–1996
SCENIC DESIGN ASSISTANT	Woodstock, NY Repertory Theater	1993–1995
ASSISTANT MANAGER	MGM Studios, Orlando	1988–1992

Education

B.A., Theater Arts - Design & Technical	San Jose State University, CA	1994

Pat Jones 77 Boxer Street Pasadena, TX 77501 713/ 477-1234
◆◆◆◆◆◆

Summary: Position in Travel Agency or Cruise Line; willing to relocate
- Experienced in air/land/cruise travel arrangements.
- Excellent organization and interpersonal skills.
- Extensive relationships with hotels, cruise lines, resorts.
- First-hand experience with many European, Caribbean locales.
- Fluent in French, German and Italian.

Professional Experience:

◆Cruise Sales Agent
CRUISE WORLD Houston, TX   1990 to present
Cruises booked for Atlantic and Pacific coasts.

FLORIDA CRUISELINE Orlando, FL   1988 to 1990
Cruise vacations arranged between East Coast locations and Florida Coast.

◆Travel Consultant
SUNSHINE TRAVEL Orlando, FL   1987 to 1988
Specialized in travel to southern France, Italy, Spain.

◆Travel Counselor
ADVENTURE TRIPS Ft. Meyers, FL   1986 to 1987
Arranged outdoor adventure trips around the world.

◆Reservations Agent
DRAKE'S TRAVEL AGENCY Houston, TX   1986
Trips to Mexico, Florida, Baja California and Texas

Education / Training:
Certificate - Cruise Counselor
CRUISE AGENTS INTERNATIONAL Association (CAIA)   1988

Associate Degree in Travel & Tourism Business Management
TEXAS STATE UNIVERSITY - Houston, TX   1988

- Automated Airline Reservations (SABRE)
- Internship at Travel Agency School - Houston, TX

Certificate - Travel Agent Training Program
SAN JOSE COMMUNITY COLLEGE -San Jose, CA   1986

Organizations:
American Organization of Travel Consultants
Association of Travel Agents

PAT JONES

PAT JONES
77 BOXER STREET
LAS VEGAS
NEVADA 89117
(702) 477-1234

PROFESSIONAL OBJECTIVE:

POSITION AS TRAVEL CONSULTANT OR TOUR OPERATOR
- ❏ FOUR YEARS' EXPERIENCE BOOKING TOURS IN NEVADA, CALIFORNIA AND THE FAR WESTERN STATES.
- ❏ HAVE TRAVELED EXTENSIVELY IN FAR WEST, CANADA, MEXICO.
- ❏ FLUENT IN SPANISH.
- ❏ EXCELLENT MANAGEMENT AND ORGANIZATION SKILLS.

WORK EXPERIENCE:

TOUR COORDINATOR, *MOUNTAIN TOURS, INC. LAS VEGAS, NV*

RESPONSIBILITIES INCLUDE BOOKING TOURS, ORDERING & COLLECTING TOUR BUSES, MEET AND GREET SERVICES, FLIGHT OPERATIONS AND GROUND TRANSPORTATION.
INITIATED *"WESTERN MYSTERY TOURS"* IN 1994

SUCCESSFULLY ARRANGED TOURS FOR OVER 1,800 INDIVIDUALS FOR THE PAST 12 MONTHS.

HANDLED GROUPS FROM 25 TO 300 PERSONS FOR 1/2 DAY TO MONTH-LONG TRIPS.

1992–PRESENT

SALES/RESERVATIONS, *DESERT SUN LIMOUSINE, DENVER, CO*

DUTIES INCLUDE SALES AND MARKETING, GENERATING NEW ACCOUNTS, RESERVATIONS AND BOOKKEEPING.
1992

RECEPTIONIST, *LAW FIRM OF DELUCA & DEAN, LAS VEGAS, NV*

RESPONSIBILITIES INCLUDE HEAVY PHONE OPERATION, LEGAL FILING & INVOICING, COMPANY CORRESPONDENCE & SCHEDULING APPOINTMENTS.
1991

ACADEMIC PREPARATION:

BACHELOR OF ARTS

UNIVERSITY OF NORTHERN COLORADO, GREELEY, CO
1990

PAT JONES
77 BOXER STREET
BEDFORD MANOR, NY 10687
(914) 477-1234

JOB OBJECTIVE: A Management Position in Television Programming or Production

EXPERTISE:

- ▲ Station programming.
- ▲ Off-line editing of news, entertainment, talk and special events.
- ▲ Facility and systems design.
- ▲ Overseeing day to day operations.
- ▲ Staff, budgets and facility management.

ACCOMPLISHMENTS:

Developed news department for Channel 12 Westchester.
Designed production facility for ChannelNET that included state of the art control room, studio, automated master control, on-line edit suite and off-line rooms.
Edited various news programs, live multi-camera remote concerts for MTV, music videos, talk, public affairs programs and station promos.
Managed staff of 120 and responsible for a budget in excess of $3M.

WORK HISTORY:

1992–Present	Channel 12 Westchester Program Director	Dobbs Ferry, NY
1986–1992	ChannelNET Assistant Facility Manager	Doddswood, NY
1983–1985	MTV-Saturday Night Freelance Director Videotape Editor	New York, NY

EDUCATION:

Emerson College	Boston, MA Bachelor of Fine Arts

AWARDS:

Cable Ace Award
Sunset Video Festival - First Prize, Long Format

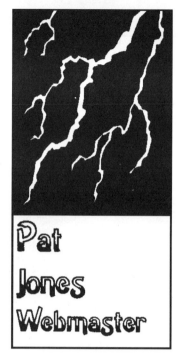

Pat Jones Webmaster

77 Boxer Street
Bedford Hills, NY
10516-1703
(914) 477-1234
E-Mail pjones@jones.com
http://www.patj/jones.com
http://www.tryus.com

Objective:
Computer/network
professional seeks position in growing
Internet-based
company desiring a strong, creative
presence on-line.

I can offer excellent
technical and creative abilities,
strong leadership, customer service,
computer and troubleshooting skills.

Experienced on
Windows 3.1
Windows95
OS/2

ACCOMPLISHMENTS

⇨ Wrote and graphically designed websites for local businesses and organizations.
⇨ Designed web pages using HTML, JAVA, and Shockwave.
⇨ Conducted research to locate visual graphics and usable links.
⇨ Configured Internet software applications
⇨ Oversaw the activities of 6 employees and establish production and programming schedules, as well as designing training programs.
⇨ Part of CAD team that generated $3.5 million in savings.

EXPERIENCE

3/95–Present
Lead Computer System Administrator
IBM, Inc.
Purchase, New York

3/95–Present
Designer / Web Page Design
WebPagers, Inc.
Somers, NY

SKILLS

Internet Applications:
Netscape 2.0, 3.0, and GOLD, Microsoft Explorer,
Pine Mail, Telnet, FTP, HTML, JAVA, Shockwave,
EudoraLite.

Word Processing:
Microsoft Word, Word Perfect

Desktop Publishing:
Microsoft Works, Microsoft Publisher

Graphics:
Corel Draw, Adobe Photoshop, Print Shop, CAD

Education

Westchester Community College
Valhalla, NY
1994–Present

Visit my web sites
Ask to see my portfolio

Pat Jones

77 Boxer Street   New York, New York 10012
E-mail: pjones@jones.com

WRITER-PRODUCER-DIRECTOR

[212]477-1234
Fax[212]477-1234
Cellular [999]477-1235

SUMMARY: Over 20 years' experience writing, producing and directing TV commercials, films, made for TV movies, videos. Computer literate, PC, Internet.

SKILLS:

Casting	Organizing	Dealing with unions	Producing
Directing	Scheduling	Analyzing stories	Researching
Writing	Budgeting	Managing Production	Photographing

WORK HISTORY:

PAT JONES PRODUCTIONS   **1980–Present**
New York City

Freelance Production Services

J. Allen Productions	Williams & Evans Agency	Bob Wisher
Forever Yours, Inc.	Watkins Agency	Retro Films Company
Q1, Incorporated	Newell, Best & Chambers	ShowTime
New Media Films	Black Rock Productions	Archival Film Forum

Highlights: Q1 Productions *"Parallel Universe,"* Showtime Original, Mel Gibson Producer.
Original screenplay, *"Last Date. First Love,"* Miramar Films.
Wrote successful long-term business plan for start-up production company (Ethan Hawke & Claire Danes).
Successfully established NY office for Toronto-based FILMSQUAD.
Numerous TV Commercials. Agency/Client List Available.

WALTER EVANSON   **1970–1979**
New York City
Senior TV Commercial Producer.
TV Business Manager.

AFFILIATIONS:

Directors Guild of America (DGA).
Member, Director's Associates.
Co-Editor, *SCRIPTERS,* Newsletter.
Independent Feature Project (IFP).
FreeLance Producers Network (FPN).

EDUCATION:

B.S., Advertising, Fairleigh Dickinson University.
Numerous Film and Writing Courses and Seminars.

Index

Other Books by the Authors

201 Answers to the Toughest Job Interview Questions
How to Get a Job in 90 Days or Less

To order, please write:

> The McGraw-Hill Companies
> Customer Services
> P.O. Box 545
> Blacklick, OH 43004-5645

Or call: 1-800-722-4726

Or fax: 1-614-755-5645